TAMING YOUR
AMYGDALA

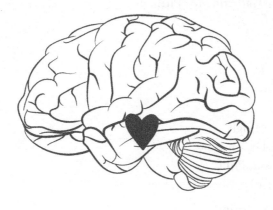

Brain-Based Strategies
to Quiet the Anxious Mind

Catherine M. Pittman, PhD, HSPP

Published by
PESI Publishing, Inc.
3839 White Ave
Eau Claire, WI 54703

Cover: Amy Rubenzer
Illustrations: Arrianna Leigh
Additional Graphics: Dreamstime
Editing: Jenessa Jackson, PhD
Layout: Amy Rubenzer & Alissa Schneider

ISBN: 9781683735083 (print)
ISBN: 9781683735090 (ePUB)
ISBN: 9781683735106 (ePDF)

PESI Publishing
pesipublishing.com

About the Author

 **Catherine M. Pittman, PhD, HSPP,** has been treating anxiety-based disorders in clinical practice for over 30 years. Her background is in cognitive behavioral therapy, neuropsychology, and fear-conditioning research. This makes her uniquely qualified to provide a clear understanding of neuroscience and how that informs the selection and application of successful anxiety treatment strategies.

Dr. Pittman is the author of the popular book *Rewire Your Anxious Brain: How to Use the Neuroscience of Fear to End Anxiety, Panic, and Worry* (New Harbinger Publications). She is also a professor of psychology at Saint Mary's College in Notre Dame, IN. She regularly presents workshops at national conferences and national webinars on anxiety treatment and is a member of the Public Education Committee of the Anxiety and Depression Association of America.

Table of Contents

Acknowledgments

This book is dedicated to three women who have taught me a great deal about the amygdala through their examples.

First, my mother, Mary Ann Sutphen, who carefully concealed her fears from me when I was a child, not wanting me to acquire them. She bravely put herself into situations that she found frightening, although I didn't know it at the time, and because of her I have no fear of getting in a lake or going to the library. Even though she didn't know anything about the amygdala, she tamed her own to raise her ten children to be courageous.

Second, I thank my wife, Victoria Powers, who first encouraged me to write this book for PESI and who endured many days of sitting with me in silence as I worked on the manuscript. A survivor of being orphaned and of multiple childhood traumas, Vickie joined the Air Force while still a teenager. She inspires me every day with her ability to push through pain and combat-related PTSD and yet maintain a gentle, compassionate heart despite all that she has endured.

Finally, I would like to acknowledge a very special client, whom I will not name. She has endured cancer and Parkinson's with remarkable determination and grace, always focused on learning how to push through the pain, anxiety, and limitations imposed by her condition. Her kindness and concern for others never fails. These three women have inspired me, reminding me what can be accomplished by those who rise above their fears and don't let the amygdala rule their lives.

Chapter 1

Understanding Anxiety

Everyone experiences anxiety. But few people understand the true nature of anxiety or how it is related to the emotion-producing structures in our brains that are difficult to spell, let alone comprehend. The goal of this workbook is to help you learn more about these influential parts of your brain, especially the amygdala. Whether you have posttraumatic stress disorder (PTSD), obsessive-compulsive disorder (OCD), a phobia, generalized anxiety disorder, or any other anxiety disorder, the amygdala is involved in creating the anxiety you experience.

When you are having problems with anxiety, panic, or worry, other people often don't understand what you are going through. You may not even understand it yourself. Anxiety can be a very overwhelming and confusing experience. The good news is that, compared to many other psychological disorders, anxiety disorders are better understood by mental health professionals, and once you learn to recognize what is going on when you experience anxiety, you also know how to *do something* about your anxiety.

This workbook will help you decipher what is happening in your brain and in your body (and why those processes are happening). With this knowledge, you will be able to cope much better with what you are experiencing. Even if other people tell you that your behaviors, feelings, and thoughts don't make sense, this workbook will help *you* make sense of them, and *you* are the person that matters. So many of my clients have said, "So *that's* why this is happening!" when they learn about how the brain creates anxiety. It can be such a relief to make sense of what is going on.

But knowledge alone is not enough. You also need to know *what you can do* with that knowledge. You can change the structures in your brain that create anxiety, but achieving that change requires taking a new approach to how you respond to your anxiety and worry. That's why you need this workbook—it is designed not only to help you understand your anxiety-based difficulties, but also to give you the specific tools and steps to *train your brain to respond in different ways.*

Yes, you can change your anxiety. I can't promise you a completely anxiety-free life; no healthy human being can be 100 percent free of anxiety or fear, and that wouldn't be a good thing anyway. (I personally wouldn't want to be on the roads with drivers who have no anxiety!) What I *can* do is help you to identify the goals you have in life and give you the tools you need to make sure that anxiety and worry do not keep you from achieving those goals. And that is exactly what this workbook will guide you through. By the end, you'll have a much better understanding of the meaning and purpose of anxiety, and how to manage it effectively.

Many people are familiar with the term *anxiety*, but they may not know all the different ways it can appear in people's lives. Some people feel nauseous, some tremble, some get headaches, and some just feel like running away. While we each have our own unique way of experiencing anxiety, the root cause of our anxiety is the same: the **amygdala**. This is the part of your brain that controls the anxiety or fear response. If you want to manage your anxiety, the amygdala is the most important part of the brain to understand. Although the responses that the amygdala creates are designed to protect you, the responses may not fit the situation. Most of these responses prime your body to fight or flee from a potential predator or threat, but fighting and fleeing are often not appropriate responses in the twenty-first century. Fortunately, certain aspects of the anxiety or fear response can be changed. In this workbook, you will learn a variety of ways to tame your amygdala so you can change your anxiety.

Rating Your Anxiety

The first step you can take if you want to change your anxiety is to simply measure it. That way, you can better recognize your anxiety and observe how it changes from day to day and in different situations. In some situations and on some days, it will be stronger, and if you keep track of it, you may be able to discern why it changes. You will also get a better understanding of the different dimensions of your anxiety. Measuring your anxiety can help you become more aware of what is happening in your body when the amygdala activates the anxiety or fear response, which will help you in the following ways:

1. **Becoming more aware of your specific anxiety symptoms can help you manage how you react to them.** Anxiety is designed to be an uncomfortable and distressing experience, so it is easy to simply react to it negatively, without awareness. You may not notice that the muscles in your back and shoulders are very tense, or recognize that your headache is due to muscle tension. You may also misinterpret feelings of nausea and think you are ill, rather than anxious. Becoming aware of the physical aspects of anxiety will allow you to have greater control over how you react to your anxiety, and it will open up more opportunities for controlling the anxiety response itself.

2. **Identifying your specific symptoms can help you recognize the evolutionary purpose behind them and normalize them.** Anxiety is part of an evolutionarily adaptive **defense response** that was designed with one important purpose in mind: to protect us from danger. The defense response (also called the stress response) protected our ancestors from dangers like wild animals or other predators by prompting them to run away from, fight against, or hide from these threats. People without fear or worries were less likely to survive or make sure their children survived. Therefore, humans alive today are likely to be the descendants of the frightened people, not the calm people!

Even though most of the concerns we face in our modern lives are different, we still have that built-in defense response that creates anxiety. Having more awareness of the symptoms you experience will help you notice the evolutionary benefit of the anxiety response reflected in many of your symptoms. For example, when you are anxious, your heart may start to pound. This makes sense when you understand that the amygdala is preparing the body to run away by pumping blood more strongly into your arms and legs. Even though anxiety can be distressing, it is a normal operation of the human brain. Everyone has anxiety to some degree, and the goal is not to eliminate it completely but to make sure it doesn't limit your life.

3. **Recognizing how your anxiety changes in response to different situations can help you pinpoint your anxiety triggers and recognize other useful factors.** Everyone's anxiety changes from moment to moment, as well as from day to day. By taking repeated measurements of your anxiety symptoms, you can begin to recognize that your anxiety is associated with certain triggers, like particular sounds, situations, or thoughts. Certain aspects of your life, like sleep and exercise, can also affect your anxiety. You may notice as well that your anxiety tends to occur at certain times of the day. By measuring fluctuations in the frequency and intensity of your anxiety symptoms, you can develop an awareness of the various factors that influence your anxiety.

On the next page, you will find a worksheet that gives you a way to quickly assess your anxiety. Please complete it a couple of times per day for a week or so to get an idea of how you experience anxiety. Remember, no one experiences anxiety just like you do. Even though there are common aspects of anxiety, everyone experiences it differently.

Rating Your Anxiety

This survey is an adapted version of the Hamilton Anxiety Rating Scale (Maier et al., 1988); you can use it to measure your anxiety and get a better idea of your specific anxiety symptoms. Anxiety involves more than just your mood, and this survey breaks down anxiety into several different dimensions that can impact you. It will help you become more familiar with and perhaps less overwhelmed by the different aspects of your anxiety. Some symptoms may surprise you, as you may not have realized they could be associated with anxiety.

Use the following scale to rate the intensity of each aspect of your anxiety at the present time. At the end of the survey, you will add up your scores to get an overall rating of your current anxiety.

0 = Not present   1= Mild   2 = Moderate   3 = Severe

_____ 1. **Anxious mood** (worries, anticipating the worst, fearful anticipation, irritability)

_____ 2. **Tension** (muscle tightness, fatigue, startle response, moved to tears easily, trembling, restlessness, inability to relax)

_____ 3. **Fears** (of the dark, strangers, being left alone, animals, insects, traffic, crowds, illness, etc.)

_____ 4. **Insomnia** (difficulty falling asleep, broken sleep, early awakening, unsatisfying sleep and fatigue upon waking, dreams, nightmares, night terrors)

_____ 5. **Intellectual effects** (difficulty concentrating, problems focusing, poor memory)

_____ 6. **Depressed mood** (loss of interest, lack of pleasure in hobbies, sadness, emotional numbness, early waking, feeling worse in the morning)

_____ 7. **Somatic/muscular symptoms** (pains and aches, twitching, stiffness, muscle jerks, grinding teeth, unsteady voice, increased muscle tone)

_____ 8. **Somatic/sensory symptoms** (ringing in ears, blurred vision, hot and cold flashes, feelings of weakness, prickling sensations, dizziness, metallic taste)

_____ 9. **Cardiovascular symptoms** (rapid heartbeat, pounding heart, fluttering heart, throbbing of vessels, feeling of pain in the chest, missing a beat)

_____10. **Respiratory symptoms** (pressure or constriction in the chest, choking feelings, sighing, difficulties breathing, tendency to hold one's breath)

_____11. **Gastrointestinal symptoms** (difficulty swallowing, abdominal pain, burning sensations, abdominal fullness, nausea, vomiting, gurgling stomach, loose bowels, diarrhea, loss of weight, constipation)

_____12. **Genitourinary symptoms** (frequency of urination, urgency of urination, no period, heavy or prolonged periods, difficulties with orgasm, premature ejaculation, loss of interest in sex, difficulties maintaining erection or ejaculating)

_____13. **Autonomic symptoms** (dry mouth, flushing, paleness, tendency to sweat, giddiness, tension headache, raising of hair)

_____14. **Behavior** (fidgeting, restlessness or pacing, tremor of hands, furrowed brow, strained face, sighing or rapid breathing, repeated swallowing, avoidance)

Now total all the numbers that you wrote for each of the 14 items. This will give you an overall anxiety score for this situation/time: _____

What Does Your Anxiety Score Tell You?	
0–13	Minimal anxiety
14–21	Mild to moderate anxiety
22–35	Moderate to severe anxiety
36–42	Severe anxiety

It is a good idea to use the anxiety scale more than one time per day and to make a habit of recording both the date and time for each score. It is also helpful to record what was happening at the time you completed the scale so you can become more aware of what triggers your anxiety. Details like this make it a more useful record. You may want to get a personal journal, so you have plenty of space to write your anxiety scores (and other helpful notes), or you can make copies of the **Record of Daily Anxiety** provided on the next page.

If you aren't interested in monitoring your anxiety, or if you find that too much assessment increases your anxiety, you don't need to keep this record longer than a week or so. However, I encourage you to retake this assessment periodically as you work through the various exercises and tools in this workbook. As you begin to try different coping strategies, keeping this record will allow you to see how different strategies affect your anxiety score and how much you are improving, so you can determine which tools are most effective in reducing your anxiety.

Record of Daily Anxiety

Use this worksheet to keep track of your anxiety scores over time, as well as to make note of any potential triggers associated with your anxiety. Be sure to use the survey from the **Rating Your Anxiety** worksheet to calculate your score for each instance of anxiety.

An example has been started for you first, followed by a blank template to record your own anxiety scores.

Date	Time	Anxiety Score	Triggers or Other Notes (What was happening at the time?)
10/25	7:30 P.M.	16	Had a difficult conversation with my partner; anticipation of the worst (breakup)
10/26	10:00 A.M.	25	Received an email from my boss about an unexpected work assignment

Date	Time	Anxiety Score	Triggers or Other Notes (What was happening at the time?)

Chapter 2

Meet Your Amygdala

The part of your brain that sends the signals to produce anxiety is small enough to fit in the palm of your hand. The amygdala is roughly the size and shape of an almond. In fact, the word **amygdala** (pronounced "uh-MIG-da-la") comes from the Greek word for almond. You actually have two amygdalae, one on each side of your brain. However, the tradition is to refer to this paired structure in the singular, so I will discuss "the amygdala" in this workbook.

If you want to show someone where your amygdala is, you can use your index fingers to point it out. Just point your right index finger at your right ear and your left index finger at your right eye. The location where the lines from these two fingers meet is about where your right amygdala is situated in your brain. (You could do the same thing, but mirrored, to point to your left amygdala.) The amygdala is located deep within the brain and has connections to some very influential brain structures located in that same area, like the brainstem, hypothalamus, hippocampus, and ventral striatum, as well as arousal networks that affect the cortex (LeDoux, 2015). The interconnections between these brain regions allow the amygdala to create your physical experience of fear—changing your emotions, thoughts, attentional focus, and various bodily functions in a fraction of a second.

What's more, these changes occur without your control and mostly outside of your awareness. It's for this reason that we often describe the amygdala as having the ability to "hijack" the brain and take charge over how we think and feel. This explains why we often don't understand our emotional reactions and why it sometimes feels like our emotions are "out of control." You don't have much control over what your amygdala does, although you can learn some ways to influence it if you learn more about how it functions (Pittman & Karle, 2015).

At its core, the amygdala is a small but powerful part of your brain designed to assist you in detecting, avoiding, defending against, and surviving dangers. (The amygdala actually does more than this, but we will focus on these functions because they relate to the amygdala's role in producing anxiety.) In particular, the amygdala is in charge of initiating a preprogrammed defensive reaction (LeDoux, 2015) that is found not just in humans, but in all animals. When it triggers this built-in reaction in our bodies, we often refer to the entire reaction as *fear* because fear is the emotional state that we are experiencing. But the reaction the amygdala creates involves many more processes in our bodies besides the emotion of fear, including the inhibition of stomach activity, an increase in blood flow to the extremities, and the release of adrenaline. What we are really experiencing is a defensive motivational state, a collection of changes in our bodies that prepare us to take actions intended to protect us.

This defensive motivational state is what produces anxiety, which is very similar to the feeling of fear. When we can identify a clear and imminent danger, like a dog that is growling or a car that is speeding toward someone crossing the street, we use the term **fear** to describe the emotion that the amygdala creates. In contrast, when we feel this emotional state when no clear danger exists, just the potential for a future threat or negative outcome—for example, when we are worrying about an upcoming exam or dreading the awkward conversation on a first date—we call the emotion **anxiety**. Whether you are feeling fear, anxiety, dread, or a similar emotion, your body is in that defensive state produced by the amygdala, a state also called the fight-or-flight response.

One problem with this preprogrammed defense response is that the dangers it was designed to protect you against have been successfully eliminated in most parts of the world. For example, you probably are not at risk of being eaten by a predator as you go about your daily life. But your amygdala is still on the lookout for dangers like this. Therefore, the stressors of today's world—like difficulty paying the mortgage or a potential argument with your boss—still elicit a defensive reaction from your amygdala that is intended to help you fight or run away from the threat. That is why your heart rate increases and your muscles tense up. These responses are typically not helpful because they don't fit the situation. You can't run away from your mortgage, and it wouldn't be wise to hit your boss. The defensive reaction may help us escape true physical dangers every once in a while, but it doesn't provide an advantage in most of the situations you face.

You will come to recognize that your amygdala often creates a defense response (including the feeling of fear or anxiety) on the basis of incorrect or insufficient information. One way to look at it is to say that the amygdala has good intentions but often produces unnecessary anxiety and takes us along for the ride. And it is not a very pleasant ride! However, you can learn how to gain more control over this small part of your brain that has such an important impact on your life.

Is Every Amygdala the Same?

Now that you know more about the amygdala and its influence, you might be wondering whether different people have the same kind of amygdala. Do some people have an amygdala that reacts more strongly or more frequently, causing it to produce more anxiety and fear than the average person's amygdala? The answer is yes: We have discovered that some people—and even some horses, dogs, and mice—have an amygdala that is more likely to produce fear or anxiety. For example, children with anxiety disorders have been shown to exhibit differences in their amygdala compared to children without anxiety disorders (Milham et al., 2005). These differences in anxiety often become apparent during the first months of children's lives, when we notice that some are more easily startled or frightened.

Studies have shown that these differences are partly a result of genetic influences, meaning that difficulties with anxiety tend to run in families (Hariri et al., 2005; Havinga, 2020). Therefore, if you struggle with anxiety, it is likely that other members of your family suffer from anxiety too, although perhaps in different ways. However, as you will learn in chapters 9 and 10, the amygdala is capable of learning to respond differently, so the amygdala you are born with does not have to determine your destiny. For example, many shy and anxious children grow up to be effective public speakers and performers.

But genetics aren't the only reason why people are anxious. Many people who don't seem anxious in their early lives can develop anxiety difficulties later on. The fact that the amygdala is capable of learning also means that some people have an amygdala that learns to produce anxiety in more situations than it once did. The amygdala learns from our specific life experiences, and it responds to objects, situations, and events that have been associated with negative events. For example, if you are in a car accident, you may begin to have anxiety when riding in a car. Suddenly, anxiety is a more limiting factor in your life than it was before.

When the event is very threatening and considered traumatic, the amygdala may be even more severely affected. After a traumatic life experience, changes occur in the amygdala that cause it to produce more anxiety in general, not just in situations associated with the trauma (Cacciaglia et al., 2017). But even though your amygdala may have learned to produce more anxiety or to produce anxiety in situations it never reacted to before, it can also learn to respond differently again if it is given the right kind of "lessons." Although you can't fully control the brain you inherited or every life experience that comes your way, you can focus on increasing your resources for taming your amygdala. You should be the one in charge of your life, not your amygdala.

How Can I Have More Influence Over My Amygdala?

You can influence your amygdala in two key ways. First, you can focus on changing your amygdala's general level of reactivity by targeting aspects of your daily routine that research has shown to have an impact on how the amygdala responds. In other words, you can tame your amygdala by living your life in a way that makes the amygdala generally calmer. Second, you can work on teaching your amygdala to respond differently in specific situations by providing it with new information about these situations, an approach called *exposure*. Most people find that teaching the amygdala is more challenging because it requires exposing the amygdala (and themselves) to situations in which they typically experience anxiety. Combining these two approaches of calming and teaching the amygdala is the most effective way to tame it.

The first approach, changing some of your habits in your day-to-day routine may be the best place to start taming the amygdala. In fact, I will let you in on some very helpful information that has only been discovered in the last 15 years or so: *The amygdala's functioning is influenced by some daily habits that you can change for very little cost and in ways that have surprising calming benefits for the amygdala.* These habits include your sleep, exercise, and diet. When you begin by changing these habits, you will find that the second step, teaching the amygdala to respond differently, is easier because you are working with a calmer amygdala.

Later in this workbook, I will guide you through these two steps in more detail. Before you begin the challenging process of changing your amygdala, however, it's important to make sure that you are motivated and well-prepared for the work ahead of you. Therefore, the next chapter will focus on your goals in life. Typically, the reason people want to tame their amygdala is because they feel like anxiety is keeping them from living the life they want. It is essential that you clarify what you hope to accomplish in your life so you can determine how anxiety may be interfering with those goals—and, ultimately, how you can overcome your anxiety to achieve your goals.

Chapter 3

Goal Setting: The First Step to Taking Your Life Back

As you may remember, it is not possible to rid yourself of all anxiety. Instead, we are looking to manage it. To do this, you must *identify the goals you have in life and acquire the tools necessary to make sure anxiety and worry do not keep you from achieving those goals.* In this chapter, you'll explore how feelings of anxiety, nervousness, worry, dread, caution, fear, or panic have interfered with your goals in life, and you'll have an opportunity to select goals you want to achieve despite anxiety. You do not have to give up on your goals and allow the amygdala to run your life.

A good place to start is to consider your daily life. When you get up each day, do you have specific thoughts about what you want to do, or do you jump right into the day's activities? Perhaps you have a list of what you *should* do each day that is actually quite demanding. No matter how you approach your day, you have certain expectations for what you will do, which we will call your goals. Sometimes these daily goals are blocked by anxiety, worry, or panic.

Impact of Anxiety on Your Daily Life

Throughout this chapter, you will find prompts that will help you reflect on how anxiety has interfered with your life. You can write your answers on these pages, or you can use additional paper or a journal if you need more space. More than one idea may come to you for each prompt.

If it weren't for my anxiety, I would like to…

_____

_____

_____

_____

_____

My anxiety and worry keep me from…

_____

_____

_____

_____

_____

Because of my anxiety or worries, I don't go…

_____

_____

_____

_____

_____

When I feel anxiety, I stop trying to…

_____

_____

_____

_____

_____

It may be difficult for you to consider daily goals you'd like to accomplish because you feel anxiety at the very thought of doing some activity or being in certain situations. You may even find that you avoid considering these scenarios. This is one of the most limiting aspects of your amygdala: It causes you to stop thinking about potential goals because the amygdala produces anxiety when you even have thoughts about certain activities. This anxiety response often arises after a traumatic event. For example, you may have enjoyed shopping at local stores, but after being in a car accident, you now find yourself having difficulty driving anywhere because of the anxiety associated with driving. As a result, you may not even think about shopping anymore because that would require you to drive.

To get around this dilemma and pinpoint your goals, consider what you *used* to do in your everyday life so you can identify what anxiety, dread, worry, or panic is blocking you from even considering.

Before I had such problems with anxiety, I used to…

_____

_____

_____

_____

_____

Before all this, I remember that I once really enjoyed…

_____

_____

_____

_____

_____

My friends wonder why I no longer…

_____

_____

_____

_____

_____

I really miss being able to…

_____

_____

_____

_____

_____

One way my life has changed due to anxiety is that I don't...

_____

_____

_____

_____

_____

Now look back over what you have written, and begin to identify some goals for your life that you would like to work toward.

Some goals I would like to try to accomplish in my life are...

_____

_____

_____

_____

_____

Impact of Anxiety on Your Relationships

Another way to identify how anxiety may be limiting you is to consider your relationships with your family, friends, and coworkers. What would you like to be doing with people in your life that anxiety prevents you from accomplishing? What types of fun are you not participating in? What kinds of interactions did you once have that you now avoid? In considering these questions, you may find that your anxiety is impacting your relationships in surprising ways.

For example, after a tumultuous and argumentative dating relationship, Brittany found that she no longer enjoyed debating with coworkers or standing up for herself in arguments with her sister. She now felt anxious at the hint of conflict and worried constantly about offending or irritating others. Similarly, consider Joe, who turned down an invitation to hang out with a group of friends because he experienced anxiety when interacting in unstructured groups. Joe missed opportunities to make new friends and to spend time with the few friends he did have.

Consider how your relationships and interactions with coworkers, family, and friends have been affected by anxiety. Remember, you can write more than one answer to a prompt, especially if you respond differently around different people or in different situations.

Though it once didn't bother me, I find myself anxious when people...

_____

_____

_____

_____

_____

I wish I could do this with others...

_____

_____

_____

_____

_____

My anxiety interferes in my relationships because I don't...

_____

_____

_____

_____

_____

When my family or friends invite me, I wish I could...

_____

_____

_____

_____

_____

I often think about saying something but don't when I am around...

_____

_____

_____

_____

_____

If it weren't for my anxiety, other people would see me doing or being...

_____

_____

_____

_____

_____

I could have a lot more fun with _____ by doing or going...

_____

_____

_____

_____

_____

I would like to be able to say or explain to _____ that...

_____

_____

_____

_____

_____

In my romantic relationship, I would like to...

_____

_____

_____

_____

_____

My relationship with _____ would be better if I could...

_____

_____

_____

_____

_____

My anxiety keeps me from going to or participating in...

_____

_____

_____

_____

_____

In my relationships, I need more...

_____

_____

_____

_____

_____

Now look back over what you have written, and identify some goals you have for your relationships that anxiety is interfering with.

With people at work, I would like to be able to…

_____

_____

_____

_____

_____

With my partner, I would like to be able to…

_____

_____

_____

_____

_____

With my family, I would like to be able to…

_____

_____

_____

_____

_____

With my friends, I would like to be able to…

_____

_____

_____

_____

_____

For recreation and fun, I would like to be able to…

_____

_____

_____

_____

_____

Impact of Anxiety on Your Work or Career

In addition to your relationships, anxiety may be affecting your work or career in a variety of ways. For example, one of my first clients wanted to get a nursing degree, but she kept dropping out of a required class because it involved giving several speeches, and she was afraid of public speaking. This anxiety was preventing her from even beginning her desired career. Anxiety and worry can also block someone from advancing in an already established career. They may exhibit poor work performance or struggle to complete tasks in a timely manner due to anxiety.

Try to identify some specific ways that anxiety prevents you from being more successful at work.

If it weren't for my anxiety at work, I would…

_____

_____

_____

_____

It would improve my performance at work if I could…

_____

_____

_____

_____

My anxiety keeps me from advancing because I can't seem to...

_____

_____

_____

_____

_____

My anxiety impairs my time management by...

_____

_____

_____

_____

_____

My advancement is limited because I turn down opportunities to...

_____

_____

_____

_____

_____

Now look back over what you have written to see where anxiety interferes, and identify some goals you have for yourself at work.

At work, I would like to be able to...

_____

_____

_____

_____

Taking Back Control of Your Life from Your Amygdala

After completing the prompts in this chapter, you can more clearly recognize how anxiety is negatively affecting certain aspects of your life. It's important to remember that the amygdala developed in primitive humans who lived in very different situations, and its responses are not always appropriate for the life you are living today. That's why you need to make sure your own *goals* direct your life, not the defensive processes produced by your amygdala. Now is the time to look honestly at any goals you have been unable to pursue or achieve due to the anxiety produced by your amygdala. Focusing on specific goals is a good way to start exploring how to take back your life from the limiting effects of anxiety.

Important Goals

This worksheet will help you select some goals for yourself and then rate these goals on two different dimensions—importance and anxiety—to determine which goals you should focus your efforts on.

First, review the goals you wrote in response to the previous prompts in this chapter—the things you want to accomplish in your daily life, your relationships, and your work or career. A good way to state a goal is to start with a phrase like "I would like to" or "I would like to be able to." If you find yourself writing out quite a few goals and feel overwhelmed, know that you are simply writing them down—you aren't committing yourself to *all* of these goals, just considering possibilities.

Next, use a scale of 1 to 10 to rate the *importance* of each goal, giving a higher score to goals that are more meaningful or beneficial to you. For example, Joshua might have one goal to be more comfortable around dogs and another goal to be calmer and more confident driving on the expressway. He rates the importance of being comfortable around dogs as a 5 because the aim of this goal is to occasionally visit the home of a friend who has a Siberian husky. However, he rates his goal about driving on the expressway as a 9 because it's more important to him that he stop wasting time driving less-direct routes to work every day. Make sure to use your *own* perspective on what is important; while you may consider what other people want you to do, you should ultimately decide which goals are most meaningful to *you*.

Then use a scale of 1 to 10 to rate the level of anticipated *anxiety* associated with each goal, with higher scores reflecting greater levels of anxiety. If you find it difficult to rate your anxiety for a particular goal because it depends on the situation, you may want to write it as two separate goals. For example, Joshua works the afternoon shift, and he feels a lot of anxiety when driving to work in midday traffic—definitely a 9 or 10. But when he comes home late in the evening when the traffic is lighter, it is only a 6. Joshua could write one goal about driving to work and another goal about driving home.

Goal achievement is often best accomplished in a gradual or step-by-step process, so whenever you feel like a goal can have differing levels of anxiety depending on the circumstances, it is helpful to make separate goals.

Goal *(I would like to… or I would like to be able to…)*	Importance (1–10)	Anxiety (1–10)

Listing your goals and rating them in this manner is an important accomplishment. You may notice that just *thinking* about your goals causes you to feel some anxiety, so as you push through that anxiety to consider these goals, give yourself credit! You are taking the first steps toward living a life that is focused on your own aspirations and not governed by your amygdala. You are not allowing anxiety to block you.

Now you are ready to choose the goals you want to work on first. As you review each goal on the previous worksheet, consider the level of anxiety you associated with it. Goals that result in less anxiety are easier to achieve. In fact, when people begin writing out their goals, they sometimes realize that their anxiety about a certain goal is low enough for them to begin working on it immediately. For example, when Victoria, who was recovering from a near drowning, wrote down her goal of going to the lake, she realized that it was actually the goal of *swimming* in the lake that made her anxious. She rated her anxiety about going to the lake as a 2 and then added another goal about swimming, which she rated as a 10. This realization motivated Victoria to develop a plan to visit the lake, something she had not considered possible until she began writing down her goals and rating them.

Just as some goals are easier to achieve because they cause less anxiety, other goals are challenging to accomplish because they require you to experience more anxiety. Anxiety is never pleasant, and the only reason to push yourself through the process is to achieve something that really matters to you. For this reason, I only ask my clients to put themselves through the experience of anxiety when it involves goals that are important to them. For example, Angelo is afraid to drive in a car, ride on a bus, take a train, or fly on an airplane, but the only situation that is important to him is driving a car. He has no reason to ride on a bus or train, and he would only rarely have an opportunity to fly. Not being able to drive is limiting his life, so that is the goal to focus on.

Remember that eliminating all anxiety from your life is not necessary, healthy, or possible. Instead, the point of taming your amygdala is to put you in control of your life, and the goals you select will guide this process. This is not to say you cannot add new goals once you understand how to overcome the limits of anxiety or if you develop new ambitions. For example, Ananya had no interest in overcoming her fear of dogs until she began dating Ryan, who had a Labrador retriever. Sometimes your life changes in a way that leads you to reevaluate the importance of a goal.

Review your list of goals and, based on which goals are most important to you and which can be most easily accomplished, decide where you will begin. I recommend choosing no more than three or four goals to start with. Now you are ready to learn how to achieve these goals. Keep your goals in mind while you read. We will return to your list of specific goals in chapter 9. Meanwhile, the next two chapters will help you understand the ways the amygdala creates anxiety in your brain, as that knowledge will be essential in learning effective strategies to achieve your goals.

Chapter 4

The Two Pathways to Anxiety in the Brain

Have you ever been driving down the road, when suddenly a vehicle or an animal came into the lane ahead of you? In a situation like this, a very rapid change occurs in your body. *Before you can even think*, you find yourself taking action. Perhaps you clutch the steering wheel and quickly turn onto the shoulder, or maybe you hit the brakes. Your body reacts immediately, allowing you to avoid disaster. You don't have time to think about what to do; you just do it. Or did you do it? Do you remember deciding what the best reaction was? What part of you decided what to do?

This situation is an excellent example of the amygdala in action. The amygdala is designed to detect danger quickly and help you respond to it. Things happen so quickly, in fact, that after you have been through a situation like this, you often have to take a minute to figure out what just occurred. That's because the amygdala took charge of your body before your cortex could. In this chapter, you will see that the brain is wired to allow the amygdala to take control (LeDoux, 1996, 2015). You will be introduced to two different pathways to anxiety in the brain—the amygdala pathway and the cortex pathway—and learn the role that the amygdala plays in each pathway.

The Role of the Cortex and Thalamus

As you live your everyday life—perhaps as you read this, you are also listening to music or the ambient sounds around you and enjoying the flavor and warmth of a cup of tea or coffee—all the information that is coming from your senses must be processed by your brain before you can experience it. The part of your brain that processes sensory information is your cerebral cortex, often referred to as simply the **cortex**. This is the curvy gray part of your brain that makes up the top and largest part of your brain (figure 1).

For example, when something comes into your field of vision, you don't see it until the cortex receives information from your eyes and carries out neural processes that interpret those signals from your eyes. Ironically, the part of your cortex that processes information from your eyes is at the back of your head, a place that is (inconveniently) far from the eyes. It therefore takes a bit of time for the information to be transferred, though it is still less than a second.

Figure 1

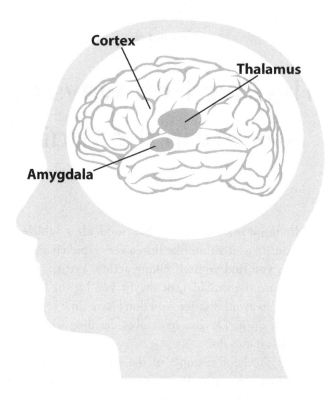

When sensory information comes into your brain—whether from your eyes, your ears, the tips of your fingers, the soles of your feet, or even your tongue—it is carried through neural pathways to the **thalamus**, a walnut-shaped area deep in the center of your brain. The thalamus is like Grand Central Station, with pathways coming in from the senses all at once. The job of the thalamus is to send incoming information on to the correct place in the brain for processing.

For example, in figure 1, you can see that sensory information from the eyes is sent from the thalamus to the occipital lobes at the back of the head. Information about what you are touching is sent from the thalamus to the parietal lobes at the top of the head; information from the ears is sent to the temporal lobes on the sides of the head; and information about what you are tasting is sent to the gustatory cortex near the center of the brain. (The only sense that the thalamus is not involved with is smell, which is processed in the olfactory cortex, a part of the brain that is located behind the nose and is directly connected to the amygdala. This is why smells can evoke such strong emotions—they go right to your amygdala.)

The thalamus also sends the information it gets from the senses directly to the amygdala, which is located relatively close to the thalamus. The amygdala gets this information more quickly than the cortex does, which means that your amygdala can process what you see, hear, feel, and taste before you consciously perceive these things, since you rely on the cortex for your sensory information. Consider the example from earlier—when the car or animal moves into the lane in front of you, the amygdala can process the visual information from the thalamus before any information has been received by the occipital lobes in your cortex. In other words, your amygdala "sees" things *before* you do (LeDoux, 1996).

The Amygdala Pathway

This very swift pathway, from the sensory receptors to the thalamus and then directly to the amygdala, gives your amygdala an advantage over the cortex (LeDoux, 1996). The amygdala can react—initiating dozens of changes in your body within milliseconds (thousandths of a second)—before your cortex has time to finish processing the information coming in from your senses. You are not consciously aware of what your amygdala sees, and it is much less detailed than what the cortex can produce, but it provides more rapid detection of potential danger. Although cortex processing takes less than a second, it cannot catch up to the speed of the amygdala. That's why it sometimes takes you a moment to be completely aware of what happened and how you responded after a threatening event. I call this pathway from the sense organs to the thalamus to the amygdala the **amygdala pathway** to anxiety (figure 2). This rapid pathway is focused on taking defensive action, and it does not rely on collecting detailed information or using logic.

Figure 2

Amygdala Pathway

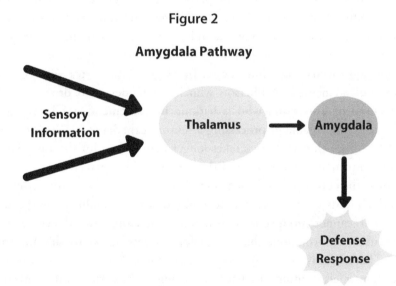

Some people mistake the amygdala's reaction for a reflex, but the underlying process is not the same. A reflex occurs when a stimulus initiates a nerve impulse that travels to the spinal cord, which then sends a direct signal back to the muscle to initiate the reflex. A reflex happens *without any part of the brain being involved*, such as when you touch a hot surface and pull your hand back quickly. When you react to a dangerous situation on the highway, your brain *is* involved, as you just learned. Information travels from the sense organs to the thalamus and then directly to the amygdala. Depending on the nature of the information received, the amygdala may create a defense response that produces many changes in your body to prepare you to react, including the physiological aspects of fear or anxiety. Understanding the nature and purpose of the defense response is essential to understanding and managing your anxiety, so we will discuss it in more detail in chapter 5.

The Cortex Pathway

The amygdala pathway is not the only avenue through which our brain can create the defense response and the ensuing feelings of fear and anxiety. A second pathway in the brain, which I call the **cortex pathway** to anxiety, can also produce these effects. If you want to be able to achieve your goals despite your anxiety, it is important to understand both pathways. Like the amygdala pathway, the cortex pathway begins with information that travels from the sense organs to the thalamus. In the cortex pathway, though, the thalamus sends the information on to the cortex. The sensory information the thalamus sends is raw and unprocessed, so it takes some time for that information to be processed, which happens in areas of the cortex called **convergence zones**. In these zones, the cortex creates a more detailed perception of the sensory information that we experience. Only after this level of processing do we consciously know what we are seeing, hearing, touching, and tasting.

The cortex allows us to perceive and interpret the meaning of information and use logic in ways the amygdala cannot. In particular, the cortex can read words, interpret complex concepts, recognize intricate details, and retrieve memories and knowledge associated with the information. For example, if you visit a friend and a big, black dog comes bounding toward you as you walk into her yard, the amygdala will see a fast-moving, large animal making a loud noise. In contrast, the cortex will recognize this dog as a Newfoundland named McPherson who has a tendency to drool and loves getting scratched behind his ears—and who is barking in excitement, not in an aggressive way. Clearly, the cortex is capable of processing a sensory experience in much more depth than the amygdala. Although this process takes longer than it does for the amygdala, it provides much more complete information about the situation being perceived.

However, the cortex pathway to anxiety does not end in the cortex itself. The defense response, which leads to emotions like fear and anxiety, is produced by the amygdala; the cortex, by itself, cannot produce these reactions. Therefore, after the cortex has processed incoming sensory information, the amygdala also gets access to this information from the cortex. That's because there are neural connections between these two brain regions, allowing the amygdala to monitor what is occurring in the cortex. If the amygdala perceives that thoughts, images, or ideas in the cortex indicate danger, it will produce a defensive motivational state, including fear or anxiety (figure 3).

Figure 3

Cortex Pathway

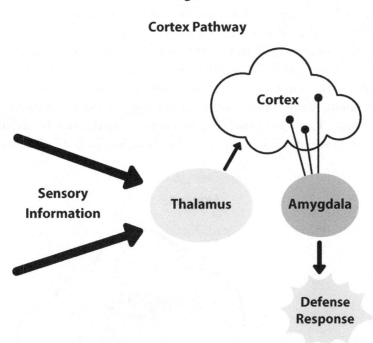

Both Pathways in Action

As you've learned, the amygdala is part of two separate pathways in the brain that can lead to anxiety. These pathways operate on different timetables and provide different levels of detail. The amygdala pathway is quicker because it transmits raw, unprocessed information from our senses; however, it doesn't have the more detailed information we are accustomed to getting through the slower cortex pathway. As noted before, you cannot perceive what your amygdala perceives, because that information is not sent to the cortex.

To better illustrate this, consider a person with cortical blindness. This condition occurs when someone has perfectly healthy eyes but cannot process visual information due to damage or dysfunction in the occipital lobes, the part of the cortex that should process this information. When information is transmitted to this part of the cortex from the eyes, nothing happens, so the person cannot see. But people who are cortically blind show awareness of movement (Sahraie et al., 1997) and can react with a startle response to something they claim they cannot see (Hamm et al., 2003). For example, if an object were coming toward the person's face, they might duck without knowing why. This is because the information from their eyes is still processed by the amygdala, even though the person has no conscious awareness of what the amygdala is processing. The amygdala can produce a defense response on the basis of information the person cannot see.

Typically, however, the amygdala pathway is not operating alone, but working in tandem with the cortex pathway. A fraternity prank can help you understand how the two pathways operate together. Daniel's fraternity brothers decided to play a joke on him by putting a plastic toy rat in the freezer to see his reaction. When they asked him to get some ice, he opened the freezer and jumped back with a shriek before uttering a string of expletives at his frat brothers that will not be printed here.

Why did this joke succeed? When Daniel opened the freezer door, his amygdala "saw" the plastic rat before his cortex did, which activated a defense response that immediately caused a variety of changes to occur in his body. However, before the shriek was completely out of Daniel's mouth, his cortex finished processing the visual information and recognized the important details: This was a plastic rat. As a result, Daniel instantly shifted to cursing out his friends, and instead of retreating from the plastic rat, he grabbed it and threw it at them (figure 4).

Figure 4

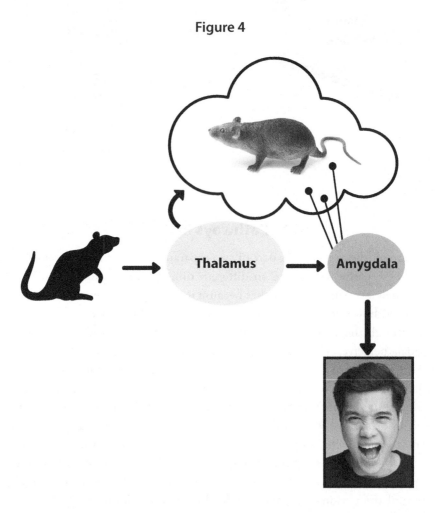

Can you see the operation of both the amygdala pathway and the cortex pathway in this example? The amygdala pathway initially caused Daniel to shriek and jump back, but then the (slower) cortex pathway provided new, detailed information that calmed the amygdala. Can you think of some examples in your own life where your amygdala caused you to react in alarm or fear, and then the cortex gave you more correct information that made you sigh in relief? You were experiencing these two different pathways in action.

If Daniel were to be honest, though, he would tell you that even after he recognized the rat was fake, he continued to experience a pounding heart, muscle tension, and a rush of adrenaline. That's because even after the amygdala stops activating the defense response, some changes in the body have occurred that cannot be canceled, and it takes several minutes for the body to return to a calm state.

Understanding the two pathways helps you recognize the amygdala's important role in producing anxiety. The amygdala involves processes that you are unaware of, and over which you have little control, which explains why you can feel anxious even when your cortex tells you that your anxiety does not make logical sense. Now, when your amygdala causes a rush of adrenaline that makes your muscles tense up and your heart start pounding, you can recognize that these sensations don't necessarily mean you are in danger, even though the amygdala is reacting as if you are. There are specific strategies you can use to influence these physical responses and calm your amygdala, as you will learn in chapters 6 through 8.

Take a moment to consider the following situations. See if you can identify whether the fear or anxiety process described can be attributed to the cortex pathway or the amygdala pathway. It helps to keep in mind which pathway is quicker, and which recognizes details. The correct answers are at the end of the chapter.

Which Pathway Is It?

1. When Marla heard the door open behind her, her heart leaped and started pounding, and she turned around quickly.

2. Tanisha heard an odd sound coming from the oatmeal boiling on the stove and recognized that the heat was too high, so she turned down the flame.

3. Tom read a text from Dave saying, "Are we going to work on putting in the garden today?" and felt nervous that Dave was getting impatient with him.

4. When Pedro tried to store his bowling ball on the shelf in the closet, it was a good thing he heard it rolling off the shelf toward his head so he could jump out of the way quickly.

5. At first, Judy wasn't concerned about the surprisingly numerous cars driving down her street, but after a couple of minutes, she decided she had better check to see why so many people were driving out of the neighborhood.

6. When Bill saw that the envelope in the mail was from the gas company, his heart sank as he remembered that he had not paid his bills this month.

7. When she finished taking the exam, Rachel found that not only were her fingers stiff from gripping her pencil, but her shoulder muscles were tight and tense. She wondered, *Why was I gripping that pencil so tightly? It wasn't trying to get away from me!*

In this chapter, you've learned that the amygdala is able to perceive and react to potential dangers before the cortex can. The brain is designed so that the amygdala receives information before the cortex does, which allows it to set in motion bodily reactions that you didn't consciously choose. Therefore, if you struggle with anxiety, it is not reflective of a lack of willpower or some other character flaw; the amygdala is not directly under your control. But the more you understand the two pathways to anxiety and how they operate, the more you can use that knowledge to influence what occurs in your brain. And by reducing the amygdala's influence, *you can reach the goals you set in life.* The first step is to learn how to communicate with your amygdala, which is the focus of the next chapter.

Answers to Which Pathway Is It?

1. Amygdala

2. Cortex

3. Cortex

4. Amygdala

5. Cortex

6. Cortex

7. Amygdala

Chapter 5

The Language of the Amygdala

In order to influence your amygdala, you need to understand its language. This means you need to know how the amygdala communicates to you, as well as how you can communicate with it. When you learn the language of the amygdala, you can understand your anxiety much better and discover ways to influence this part of your brain so it responds differently—which will allow you to work on any goals that have been blocked by anxiety.

How the Amygdala Communicates to You

As you learned in chapter 2, the amygdala does not communicate through words or thoughts but, rather, through a variety of bodily reactions. These reactions represent a preprogrammed defensive motivational state that has influenced human lives since our primitive ancestors walked the earth. These bodily reactions include increased heart rate and blood pressure, rapid breathing, dilated pupils, sudden availability of blood flow to the arms and legs, increased perspiration, and slowed digestion. In addition to these physical symptoms, people often describe experiencing emotions such as fear, dread, panic, or anxiety as part of the defense response.

Although some physical symptoms of the defense response are readily apparent, others are less obvious. For example, Frida recognized that her nausea and muscle tension were connected to her anxiety, but she didn't realize that her difficulties with paying attention were also caused by the amygdala. Therefore, if we want to understand the messages the amygdala is sending, we need to look in more detail at its preprogrammed defensive reaction. This defensive reaction is very similar in all animals, including humans, so its underlying physical processes are well-researched.

Although the defensive reaction is often known as the fight-or-flight response, researchers have discovered that the amygdala also creates a third reaction—the *freeze response* (LeDoux, 2015)—in which we are motionless or somewhat paralyzed for a period of time, not taking any action at all. This freeze response is evident in animals who remain motionless or feign death in the face of a dangerous predator. Freezing is a useful response in humans, too, and it is sometimes even more helpful than fighting or running away. For example, when Darryl's boss raised his voice and criticized him, Darryl felt a surge of panic throughout his body, but instead of responding, he just stood there rather dumbfounded. Because Darryl did not respond in a threatening manner or run away from the confrontation, his boss eventually finished his tirade and walked away. After freezing, Darryl thought through the criticism and approached his boss at a later time when they could both discuss the situation more calmly. Freezing can be beneficial, even in the modern world.

Given this third response, it is more accurate to refer to the defensive reaction as the fight-flight-freeze response (LeDoux, 2015). Your amygdala might initiate any of the three responses when you are facing a stressful situation. However, you may find that you have a more dominant tendency toward one or two of these strategies. Use the following worksheet to see whether you have a propensity to fight, flee, or freeze when the defense response becomes activated.

Do You Fight, Flee, or Freeze?

Through the defense response, the amygdala is communicating to us that we should fight, flee, or freeze. Read through the following list, and check off the statements that apply to you. Then compare the number of check marks you placed in each category to see which approach your amygdala most frequently encourages you to take.

Fighting

☐ When I am stressed, I find myself wanting to hit something or someone.

☐ When someone offends me, I feel like fighting with them.

☐ I often snap at others when they frustrate me.

☐ I throw or kick things when I am angry.

☐ When someone says something rude to me, I don't let them get away with it.

☐ I have a hard time sitting still or keeping my mouth shut in tense situations.

☐ If someone startles me, I am at risk of striking them.

☐ Sometimes I physically hurt myself rather than hurting someone else.

Fleeing

☐ I typically avoid situations that stress me out.

☐ Whenever things start to go wrong, I just want to leave.

☐ When things don't go smoothly, I have no interest in them.

☐ I have a tendency to put off things that I need to do.

☐ I will pretend I don't know about something in order to avoid addressing it.

☐ I frequently cancel activities that I planned to participate in.

☐ I often wish I could just run away from it all.

☐ I can come up with a million excuses not to do something.

Freezing

☐ I frequently find myself at a loss for words when I am stressed.

☐ When I panic, I have a hard time doing anything constructive.

☐ In difficult situations, I stay quiet and hope no one notices me.

☐ When I'm stressed, I frequently find myself unable to take action.

☐ When something is frightening, my muscles become tense and stiff.

☐ If someone startles me, I freeze and don't move.

☐ I'm slow to react or recover in a stressful situation.

☐ I shut down and feel paralyzed when someone is angry.

I prefer the term *defense response* when referring to the fight-flight-freeze response because it reminds us that the amygdala is creating a defensive motivational state intended to protect us (LeDoux, 2015). The term also helps us consider whether or not we *need* this defense, a useful consideration to keep in mind when taming the amygdala. The physical reactions involved in the defense response (e.g., increased heart rate, perspiration, slowed digestion) are accompanied by emotional experiences like anxiety, dread, or fear, but in most of the situations we experience in our present-day lives, there is no real, imminent danger—so there is no need for a defensive reaction. When you understand that the amygdala can cause you to experience these physical and emotional responses in error, or in a situation in which fighting or fleeing would not be useful, you can change your experience of these responses. This can be a complete game-changer for someone trying to combat the limiting effects of anxiety.

When you understand the language of the amygdala, you realize what is occurring in your body and brain so you don't misinterpret your reactions. For example, when your heart begins pounding and your chest feels tight, you may worry that you are having a heart attack. In reality, though, the fact that your heart is pumping faster and stronger means that it is very healthy, not that it is stopping. Similarly, if you hyperventilate and feel dizzy, you may wonder if you are unhealthy or ill, when these symptoms just reflect that the airways in your lungs are more open.

The defense response can also interfere with your thinking, especially your ability to concentrate. This is because the amygdala can take control of the cortex in such a way that we don't have access to the higher-order thinking processes that allow us to use logic or make a plan. The amygdala shapes our attention and perception by influencing what we focus on (Vuilleumier, 2009). The human brain is surprisingly limited in terms of its focus, and when you are in the grips of the defense response, the amygdala focuses your attention on whatever it considers dangerous, which keeps you from attending to other ideas or things that may be occurring. This explains why you may have difficulty coming up with step-by-step plans or processing complex ideas when you are experiencing the defense response. It also explains why test anxiety is so debilitating: A person can study for hours, memorizing all the necessary information, but then be unable to answer the test questions because thoughts of *I won't pass this test* interfere with their ability to focus on recalling that information.

Defense responses can vary from a low level of activation, in which you might feel a little sweaty but nothing else, to a full-blown panic attack, in which you feel completely overwhelmed by your symptoms and worry about dying or going crazy. When you remember that these physical, mental, and emotional symptoms are all caused by the defense response, it can reassure you that what you are experiencing is normal and that you are not having a medical problem, losing your mind, or in danger. These symptoms just reflect your amygdala preparing your body to respond to some perceived threat in the environment.

You can think of the amygdala as an alarm system against potential dangers, but alarms can go off in error. Remember that the amygdala reacts to incomplete knowledge compared to the cortex, which processes sensory information in much more detail. Therefore, the amygdala is prone to respond to benign situations as if they were dangerous.

What's confusing is that you experience the *same* reaction in both scenarios—whether the situation is truly dangerous or whether it's one in which the danger has been misinterpreted or overestimated. Of course, it is harder to question the accuracy of a *feeling* of danger than it is to question the accuracy of a mechanical alarm system, like the one in your car. The feeling of danger produced by your amygdala is more distressing. But it helps to know that just as a car alarm can go off in error, so can the amygdala.

Other people may tell you that your anxiety isn't real because it doesn't make sense to them. Of course anxiety often doesn't make logical sense! The amygdala does not operate on logic. But it is still producing a very real defense response in your body that you can't easily ignore or manage. Even if other people don't understand why you are experiencing anxiety, *you* can benefit from the knowledge that your defense response is real. You are experiencing very real emotions, bodily reactions, and thoughts in response to your amygdala's perception of danger, whether or not you are truly facing a threat in the moment.

Of course, people in these situations usually don't think to themselves, *Oh, that's just my amygdala producing a defense response.* Instead, the sensations they are experiencing often convince them that they are truly in danger. After all, they are experiencing the very same bodily reactions they would if a car were about to run over them or if a dog were about to bite them. However, if you remember that your amygdala's reactions are not always justified, needed, or the best way to respond to a situation, you can learn not to take them so seriously. After my clients learn about the defense response, they're often able to tell themselves something like "Geez, my amygdala is so jacked up right now! You would think I was facing a saber-toothed tiger instead of a quarterly report presentation."

Examining Your Own Defense Response

How exactly does the amygdala activate the defense response? The amygdala has connections to some very influential structures in the brain, including the brainstem and the hypothalamus, that allow it to create this defensive reaction. The brainstem is important in influencing arousal level and moving us into survival mode, whereas the hypothalamus initiates the release of hormones, such as adrenaline (which activates the sympathetic nervous system) and cortisol (which causes glucose to be released into the bloodstream for quick energy).

Figure 5 illustrates the remarkable changes that can occur in the body when the hypothalamus is activated by the amygdala. For example, you will likely get a dry mouth due to weakened stimulation of the salivary glands. You're also more vulnerable to hyperventilating because the airways in your lungs become more relaxed to allow you to get more oxygen. Your heart beats faster and stronger to quickly get blood to your extremities so you can fight or flee if needed. As blood is directed to your extremities, digestion slows, which can cause a feeling of nausea or stomach discomfort. Glucose is released from the liver to provide fuel for any muscle activity that is required, meaning that your blood glucose level quickly rises. You are likely to feel a rush of adrenaline and might also feel like you need to rush to the bathroom.

As you'll recall from the previous chapter, an activated amygdala has the right connections to trigger all of these physiological changes very rapidly—in a fraction of a second—before you even have time to think through how to respond to the situation. The amygdala puts your body in a position to flee or fight before your cortex has even finished processing the situation.

Figure 5

Sympathetic Nervous System

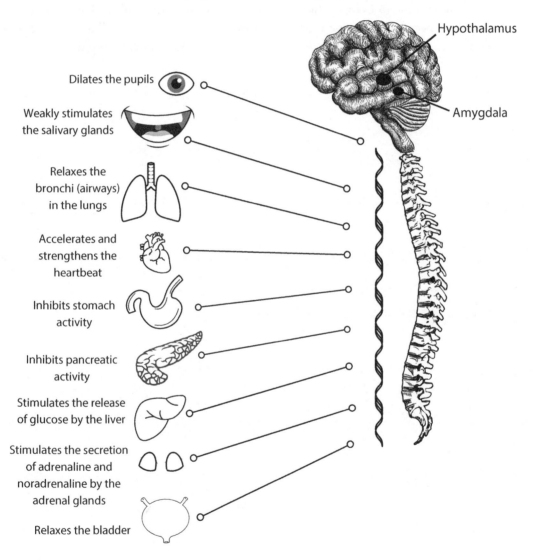

Now that you have a better understanding of the physiological changes related to the defense response, it's a good time to take a closer look at the specific nature of your own anxiety. If you have been keeping a daily record of your anxiety using the tools from chapter 1, you may already have recognized that many symptoms of your anxiety are the result of an activated amygdala. Other symptoms may seem unrelated to the defense response at first glance, but upon closer inspection—and in light of all you have learned so far—you may see a connection.

For example, it is common for humans and other animals to experience the need to urinate or to have diarrhea in response to this physiological activation. Perhaps we are supposed to empty our bowels and bladder so we can run faster? All I can say is that when I take my golden retriever to the vet, I always make sure to walk him behind the clinic before entering because otherwise, the minute they start restraining him to take his temperature, he is likely to create a big mess on the floor.

Take some time to examine figure 5 and consider how these physiological processes relate to the aspects of anxiety you see in your own life. Then use the following worksheet to help you organize your thoughts as you explore your own anxiety symptoms.

Indicators of Your Own Defense Response

Refer back to the **Rating Your Anxiety** worksheet in chapter 1. Read through the list of anxiety symptoms, and identify which of these symptoms you experience in your own life. Focus on *specific* aspects of the defense response—not general categories, like "intellectual effects," but specific symptoms within the categories, like "difficulty concentrating." There is space on this page for you to write down your symptoms.

Next, circle any of these symptoms that have been distressing to you. Perhaps you have even been worried enough to look up some of these symptoms online, but now you see that they simply reflect your amygdala in action.

Finally, for *each* symptom you circled, answer the questions that appear on the next page. You can make copies of this worksheet (or use your own journal) to reflect on all of your symptoms.

Anxiety Symptoms

Symptom: _____

What is it about this symptom that causes you to feel distressed?

_____

_____

_____

How difficult is this symptom to deal with, on a scale of 1 to 10? _____

What do you interpret this symptom to mean?

_____

_____

_____

What purpose could this symptom serve in the defense response?

_____

_____

_____

Have you been assuming that this symptom is dangerous?

_____

Have you been assuming that this symptom confirms that you are in danger?

_____

Have you been assuming that you should have control of this symptom?

_____

After learning about the amygdala, how have your thoughts about this symptom changed?

_____

_____

_____

What would be helpful for you to remember about this symptom when you experience it?

_____

_____

_____

As you've learned, people tend to misinterpret many of the changes that happen in the body and brain during the defense response, and these misinterpretations—rather than the symptoms themselves—are what often cause problems. In the previous worksheet, you identified the specific symptoms that have been increasing your anxiety and contributing to unnecessary distress, and you began to consider whether these symptoms truly mean that you are in danger—or whether your worries may result from misinterpretations of the defense response. The next worksheet will help you continue to question and challenge your anxiety. It will guide you through the process of creating effective coping thoughts that you can use to combat your worries.

How You Can Communicate with Your Amygdala

The amygdala is very capable of learning new things—if you know how to speak its language. You can't communicate with the amygdala using words or explanations. For instance, if you're riding in a friend's car during a snowstorm, trying to command your amygdala ("Calm down!") or reason with it ("Jeff is a good driver; there is no reason to be afraid") will not have an impact. The amygdala doesn't learn a thing if you simply try conversing with it; you have to approach it on its own level. Remember, the amygdala wants to create bodily reactions focused on fighting, fleeing, or freezing. It needs *experiences* to which it can react, not words.

For example, when I feel my amygdala activating the defense response, I often choose to respond in a way it understands—through exercise. I take a brisk walk, or I go on a brief run if I feel particularly stressed. When the dean asks me to come to her office for a talk, it may look like I'm hurrying across campus because I'm late for a meeting, but I'm actually giving my amygdala a calming aerobic experience (Anderson & Shivakumar, 2013). After all, the amygdala wants me to flee the situation, so when I get moving—even though I'm actually heading *toward* the dean's office—it will calm down. The situation that I feel stressed about still exists, but I'm able to calm my amygdala in spite of this (Leem et al., 2019).

Even simpler than exercising, you can use your breath to send a message to your amygdala (Jerath et al., 2012, 2015). That's because your amygdala is always paying attention to your breathing; in fact, it is able to monitor the carbon dioxide levels in your blood (Ziemann et al., 2009). If you want to create a feeling of panic, just cut off your air supply, and the amygdala will most certainly activate! The reverse is also true: if you focus on slowing your breathing, your amygdala will calm down.

Although strategies like deep breathing and exercise can help you communicate with your amygdala on its own level, perhaps it is most important to communicate *new information* to your amygdala. You can teach your amygdala that there is little danger in certain situations and that it doesn't need to create the defense response at those times. Later in this workbook, you will learn ways to teach your amygdala new information so it stops creating the anxiety that is blocking your goals. But first, let's focus in more detail on the strategies you can use to calm your amygdala.

Coping with Worries

This worksheet will help you identify and modify any worries you have been having when your amygdala activates the anxiety or fear response. In the left-hand column, use the prompt provided to write down what symptom you have been worrying about and why. Then reevaluate this worry based on your understanding of the defense response. In the right-hand column, follow the prompt to create a coping thought that can help you combat the worry.

An example is provided for you first, followed by a blank template for you to fill in with worries from your own life.

Worry	Coping Thought
"When I feel or think _____, I worry it means that _____."	"This worry may not be correct because my amygdala produces this response to try to protect me by _____."
When I feel a sense of dread, I worry it means that something bad or harmful is going to happen to me.	This worry may not be correct because my amygdala produces this response to try to protect me by focusing my attention on what it perceives as a threat, but it may not truly be a threat.

Worry	Coping Thought
"When I feel or think _____, I worry it means that _____."	"This worry may not be correct because my amygdala produces this response to try to protect me by _____."

Chapter 6

How to Calm the Amygdala

Deep Breathing

One of the first techniques I learned as a young therapist was how to train my clients in deep breathing in order to relieve anxiety. Even though a great deal of evidence has demonstrated that breathing methods are effective, I always had a difficult time convincing clients that breathing could be helpful. It just seemed too simple! Then Joseph LeDoux (1996) conducted breakthrough research showing how the amygdala is involved in creating anxiety, and new imaging technologies like functional magnetic resonance imaging (fMRI) allowed us to see the amygdala reacting in real time in the human brain (LaBar & Warren, 2009). Research showed that when individuals were placed in an fMRI machine and exposed to frightening images or negative self-beliefs, amygdala activation increased (Doll et al., 2016). However, when they were instructed to mindfully slow their breathing down while viewing or thinking about those same images or self-beliefs, amygdala activation decreased (Goldin & Gross, 2010). That changed everything! When I share these findings with my clients, they become very interested in learning breathing methods that directly affect the amygdala.

Deep breathing is an excellent strategy to keep in mind if you are regularly dealing with anxiety. In contrast to antianxiety medications like alprazolam, which can take up to 30 minutes to change the neurochemistry of the brain, breathing-focused methods can directly impact the amygdala more quickly, sometimes in as little as 10 minutes (Jerath et al., 2015). Plus, deep breathing costs nothing and is readily available to you at any time and in any location. You can use it just before your violin solo, in the middle of rush-hour traffic, or the moment after a spider unexpectedly drops in your lap.

Although a variety of deep-breathing techniques have been shown to influence amygdala activation, the most effective techniques seem to involve slow, deep breathing (Jerath et al., 2012, 2015). Slow, deep breathing activates the parasympathetic nervous system (Pal et al., 2004), which is the body's way of countering the sympathetic nervous system processes that produce the defense response. So not only are you impacting the amygdala, but you are also targeting the defense response itself. To help you practice slow, deep breathing, try the following diaphragmatic breathing exercise to see how it impacts you. You can practice this exercise whenever, but if you try it when you are feeling anxious, it will give you a better sense of whether it decreases your anxiety.

Diaphragmatic Breathing

The diaphragm is a large, curved muscle just below the lungs and the heart, and it's the primary muscle used in breathing. In order to practice diaphragmatic breathing, get into a comfortable position, either sitting or lying down. Then place one hand on your chest and one hand on your stomach, and take some full, deep breaths in, letting each breath out slowly. Your stomach should expand with each inhalation and retract with each exhalation. Sometimes it is easier to get the right response by inhaling through your nose and exhaling through your mouth, though this is not required. Breathing through pursed lips (lips that are parted just a little) can also help you slow down your breathing. Try this exercise for 10 to 15 minutes, and consider whether you feel different after that period.

When you first try diaphragmatic breathing, it may make you feel somewhat tired, as if you are using a muscle that is not in shape. That probably means you have not been getting the slow, deep breaths this type of breathing achieves, likely because you've been relying on your chest muscles rather than the more powerful diaphragm. Keep working at it, and you will learn to rely more on your diaphragm when breathing. Diaphragmatic breathing typically slows your heart rate down, although you may not notice it. Most people find it leads to feelings of relaxation.

Although diaphragmatic breathing may feel somewhat awkward at first, remember that this type of breathing is very beneficial. It allows you to get more oxygen with each breath and expel more carbon dioxide (Mendes et al., 2019). It also provides a way to turn off the sympathetic nervous system by stimulating the vagus nerve, which passes right through the diaphragm and activates the parasympathetic nervous system to turn off the defense response (Porges, 2017; Zaccaro et al., 2018).

Another breathing method that is beneficial in reducing anxiety involves long, slow inhalations that completely expand the lungs, followed by long, slow exhalations that completely empty the lungs. The exhalations seem especially important in activating the parasympathetic nervous system (Komori, 2018), which helps keep the sympathetic nervous system in check, though the point is not to extend the exhalation so much that you're holding your breath. Try the following exercise in order to pace your breathing to be deeper and slower with complete exhalations.

"Give Me Five" Breathing

This breathing technique requires you to use a clock or stopwatch at first, until you get accustomed to the right timing of your breaths. Watch the clock and try to breathe only five (or perhaps six) breaths per minute, with each breath involving a full inhalation and exhalation. This means each breath should last about 12 seconds: six seconds of inhaling followed by six seconds of exhaling. Begin by taking a deep, slow breath in, with the goal of filling your lungs to capacity. Then immediately shift to a slow, gentle breath out, making sure to completely empty your lungs. Then immediately breathe in again, slowly and deeply, to continue the process.

Remember not to hold your breath at any time. At any given moment, you should be either breathing in or breathing out. When you breathe in this slow, deep way, it doesn't matter if you breathe with your nose or your mouth. Just use the approach that works best for you. Remember to empty your lungs completely by emphasizing the out-breath. Practice lengthening your breaths until you get close to five or six breaths per minute.

Once you get into the rhythm of breathing at approximately five breaths per minute, you can add the use of imagery, which many people find helpful. This involves focusing your attention on a visual image of your breath. First, select a color that you think represents your stress or anxiety. Then imagine that you have this color of stress inside your body, but with every out-breath, you are breathing it out of yourself. Imagine it coming out of your nose or mouth like colored smoke or steam and then dissipating into the air around you. With every in-breath, imagine filling yourself up with clear, clean air and then breathing out the stress. Make sure you completely empty your lungs of every trace of that colored stress with each exhalation. Sometimes it helps if you think of a word like *calm* or *peace* as you breathe. Continue until you feel more relaxed, focusing on filling yourself with clarity and calmness.

How do you incorporate these breathing techniques so they become a part of your everyday life? First, you need to practice them enough so they become comfortable and second nature. Everyone breathes in a different way, so find the way that works for you. Don't feel that you have to breathe through your nose or purse your lips if that is not comfortable or causes some negative effects. Second, you should schedule breathing techniques into your day by practicing them at *specific* times more than once a day. If you don't put them into your schedule, or remember to use them when you feel stressed or anxious, they won't do any good. You can use them at any time—when you're in a meeting, driving, walking, or getting ready for bed. Another benefit of regular breathing exercises is that they make you more aware of when you are holding your breath, which is a common way that we often unnecessarily activate the amygdala. Remind yourself that you should always be breathing!

Although breathing exercises have been shown to reduce amygdala activation, not everyone finds deep breathing helpful. If you have asthma or other breathing difficulties, you may find that focusing attention on your breath leads to increased anxiety. But there are other effective ways to reduce amygdala activation and promote parasympathetic responding. Sometimes using imagery that has nothing to do with your breathing is more effective.

Relaxation through Imagery

Another way to calm your amygdala—and in turn, your mind—is to use imagery. With imagery, you identify a specific setting in your mind that you find relaxing and then visualize taking yourself to that location. This setting can be one that exists in the real world—such as a peaceful meadow or sunny beach that you previously visited—or it can be one that you create in your imagination.

One of my clients once asked me as he entered my office, "Are you sure you are ready to see me? Don't you get stressed by talking to several different people in a row?" I told him the reason I didn't come get him for a few minutes after the previous client was because I had taken that time to imagine myself visiting a cool, clear, and magical waterfall in the mountains. Standing in my office with my eyes closed, I imagined myself stepping into this magical water that washed away all my stress, and then I was ready to see another person. He laughed and said, "Is that what you are up to in there?" "Not always," I told him, but if I needed to, I knew I had a magical waterfall that I could visit anytime—and now he could too. If you'd like to try out imagery for yourself, try the following exercise to see how well imagery promotes relaxation for you.

Visualizing a pleasant scene can be very helpful for some people in producing relaxation. Of course, you can't always take yourself out of a situation by closing your eyes and going somewhere else in your mind. But in many cases, you'll find that taking a break and imagining yourself in a relaxing situation can calm you down and quickly recharge you. Imagery doesn't have to take a long time if you have a good imagination.

Guided Imagery

Get into a comfortable position in which you can relax. Then read through the script provided and imagine yourself in the scene. You can ask someone else to read the script to you so you can close your eyes and focus on experiencing the imagery, or you can read through it ahead of time and then close your eyes and imagine each part of the scene when you are ready. As you go through the exercise, make sure to incorporate all your senses—seeing, hearing, smelling, feeling, and maybe even tasting the situation in your mind.

You are walking in a wooded area, following a dirt road that you have been assured will lead you to a beach. As you listen to the gentle crunching of your shoes on the ground, you notice that the road is somewhat sandy, which gives you hope that the beach isn't far away. You listen to the wind gently blowing through the trees and hear the cries of seagulls. Yes! The beach cannot be far away.

As you round a curve in the shady road, you see ahead of you a sandy path that slopes away from the road and down through the trees. The trees lining the path are a mix of huge pine and oak trees, and the path is not only sandy, but also coated with pine needles from the trees. The air is filled with the fragrant smell of pines, and the wind seems to be coming up the path toward you, bringing the smell of the lake as well. You move more eagerly down the incline of the shady path and hear children's voices. Two laughing children come running up the path toward you, wearing bathing suits, their wet feet coated with sand as they run up the path.

The path becomes broader and takes you down into sunshine. You come out of the shade of the trees onto a golden beach with a clear blue lake ahead of you. You see two colorful umbrellas and a few people on the beach, but what catches your eye are the magnificent white clouds floating over the lake. Their brilliant whiteness contrasts with the light blue of the sky and the darker blue of the water. The lake is so large that you can't see the shore on the other side, just the place where the light blue sky meets the water. You stand for a moment and take in the scene, listening to the calls of the seagulls as they glide on the wind currents above the lake. You see gentle waves washing up on the shore, and you walk through the sand toward the shoreline, struggling through some of the deeper sand as you go.

As you reach the edge of the beach, you take off your shoes and shake the sand off them. You walk barefoot in the dark, wet sand near the water's edge, feeling the damp sand give gently under each step you take. You turn around and notice the footprints you are leaving in the sand behind you. Then you step toward the water to get your toes a little wet, and the coldness of the water is surprising. You don't really want to go any farther into the lake.

Still, you are very pleased to have found this beach, and as you stand and feel the waves lapping on your feet, you enjoy the sights and sounds around you. You stand and enjoy the warm sun on your shoulders and face, and the breeze off the lake moving through your hair. You take a deep breath and try to take a mental picture of the beautiful scene so you can remember it when you leave to return up the sandy trail.

Progressive Muscle Relaxation

You have learned that when the amygdala produces the defense response, one frequent symptom that results is muscle tension or trembling. Muscle relaxation strategies have been shown to counteract the effects of this amygdala activation, with progressive muscle relaxation being one of the most commonly used methods. With progressive muscle relaxation, you practice tensing and then relaxing each set of major muscle groups in your body in sequence, working to reduce muscle tension in your whole body. Although the entire process can take up to 30 minutes the first few times, once you have gotten enough practice with it, it can take less than five minutes. Most people can relax the various muscle groups quite easily, with the exception of a few, so once you learn which few muscles to focus on, the process becomes much shorter. In addition, as your body gets trained to relax, you'll find that different parts of your body begin to relax more easily.

However, some people find that tensing different muscle groups is not effective in relaxing them. This can be especially true for those with chronic pain or muscle injuries. Others just find the process annoying or tedious. If you are one of these individuals, eliminate the focus on tensing your muscles and just focus on relaxing each muscle group. Remember that your goal is to find a way to reduce the muscle tension and general level of bodily arousal created by the amygdala. By sitting with your muscles relaxed, your hands resting gently in your lap, and your palms up, you can calm yourself down more quickly than you ever could with words, especially if you focus on breathing slowly at the same time.

Try the following progressive muscle relaxation exercise to communicate a sense of safety to your amygdala by creating a sense of relaxation in your body.

Progressive Muscle Relaxation

Sit in a firm chair and begin by taking several slow, deep breaths. If deep breathing doesn't work for you, just try to keep your breathing as deep and slow as possible throughout the entire process, making sure not to hold your breath during the moments of muscle tension. You can also focus your attention on your breath by inhaling during periods of tensing and exhaling during periods of relaxation.

When you are ready, start by focusing on your **hands**. Breathe in and tense the muscles in your hands by making your hands into tight fists. You should only tense briefly, two or three seconds at the most. (Remember not to hold your breath while tensing.) Then let your hands completely relax and fall into your lap, palms up. Release any remaining tension in your hands, wiggling or shaking your fingers in order to relax them. Then breathe out and focus on the feeling of relaxation in your hands. Your muscles may feel loose and heavy, as if they are being pulled down by gravity and not resisting it.

Next, focus attention on your **forearms**. Start by briefly tightening up the muscles in your forearms, holding for a count of two or three. Then drop your hands in your lap again, and allow the muscles in your forearms to relax. Focus on releasing any tension from your elbows down, and feel the heaviness of relaxation. If you have trouble getting your muscles to relax, you can shake your arms to loosen up the muscles.

Continue this process with other muscle groups throughout your body, as listed below. Remember to only tense briefly—without holding your breath—and then relax, focusing on the heavy, loose feeling of relaxed muscles in each group.

- **Biceps:** Tense your biceps by bending your arms up to your shoulders, and then relax by allowing your arms to hang loosely at your sides.

- **Shoulders:** Tense your shoulders by pulling them up toward your ears, and then relax as you allow the weight of your arms to pull your shoulders back down.

- **Forehead:** Tense your forehead by furrowing your brow, and then relax by releasing your eyebrows back into a neutral position.

- **Mouth:** Tense your mouth by clenching your jaw, pushing your tongue against your teeth, and holding your lips together. To relax, open your mouth wide for a moment to stretch, then leave your mouth slightly open, with your tongue relaxed and your lips slightly parted.

- **Neck:** Tense your neck by tipping your head back, and then release by stretching your neck from side to side, rolling your head from left to right, ending with your chin tucked toward your chest.

- **Stomach and chest:** Tighten the muscles in your stomach and chest as if you are expecting a stomach punch, and then relax by loosening your muscles, letting them take up as much space as they need.

- **Buttocks:** Tighten the muscles in your buttocks, and then release the tension and sink comfortably into a relaxed position.

- **Calves:** Tense your calves by pushing your heels into the ground while lifting your toes, and then relax by stretching your legs out into a comfortable position.

- **Thighs:** Tense your thighs by pushing your feet into the ground, and then relax by stretching your legs out again.

- **Feet:** Tense your feet by curling your toes under, and then relax by wiggling or stretching out your toes.

When you have completed every muscle group, do a review of each group, relaxing any area that has tensed up again. Then deepen the relaxation in your entire body by relaxing into your chair and allowing your muscles to be loose and heavy. You can also use deep-breathing techniques if you wish. Repeating a word like *relax* or *peace* in your mind can also be helpful. If you do this repeatedly, your body learns to automatically relax when you say this word to yourself.

After completing this exercise, you might notice that tension tends to move back into certain muscle groups while others seem to stay relaxed. If so, you can focus your attention on the most vulnerable muscles that are in need of deliberate relaxation. With practice, most people find that they no longer need to tense each muscle, just the most stubbornly resistant ones, but remember that tensing a muscle often helps it relax more completely. You can give a resistant muscle special attention by tensing, stretching, or shaking it loosely to encourage relaxation.

When to Use These Calming Techniques in Your Daily Life

Although deep breathing, muscle relaxation, and imagery are all useful techniques that can help you manage your amygdala, there are different situations in which certain techniques may prove more effective. For example, when you are experiencing anxiety *in response to a situation or object*—such as driving on an icy road, experiencing a headache that makes you worry you have a migraine coming on, or riding in a crowded elevator—deep breathing and muscle relaxation can send a message directly to the amygdala to calm down. Because these techniques are very subtle, you can use them in the moment without others realizing it. In addition, the more you deliberately use these techniques, the more you become aware of how often you are unintentionally holding your breath or tensing your muscles. The amygdala produces a freeze response in many situations without us knowing it, and deep breathing and muscle relaxation can turn this freeze response off.

When you are experiencing anxiety in relation to some *upcoming event*, all three techniques may prove helpful. For example, if you have a job interview, you could sit for a few minutes in your car beforehand and practice guided imagery to help you feel more at ease. While imagery is not always a good strategy in situations when others are present, it can be useful in short, private moments such as this. Of course, you could also engage in progressive muscle relaxation or practice slow, deep breathing while you wait for the interview to begin.

By nature, the defense response and the associated emotions of fear and anxiety are anticipatory, meaning that they tend to occur *before* you are confronted with a threatening situation. Therefore, you will experience the highest levels of anxiety just before the stressful situation occurs. For example, someone who is *waiting* to give a speech, board a plane, or welcome guests to a party will experience greater anxiety than when they are actually giving the speech, flying on the plane, or talking with the guests. This is very counterintuitive unless you understand the defense response. Many people think, "If I feel this nervous *before* the speech, I will feel even more nervous when giving it!" But most people find that after they start talking and focusing on the speech, they calm down. From an evolutionary perspective, this makes sense. The amygdala's role is to protect you from danger, so if you experience the fight-or-flight response only after a tiger has you in its mouth, it isn't very helpful.

Another way to think of it is to picture anxiety as a hill or curve: Your anxiety steadily increases as you approach the trigger, where it peaks. Once you are in the situation, as long as nothing dangerous appears, the amygdala will produce less and less anxiety until you're back to flat ground at the bottom of the hill. Therefore, it is important to use calming strategies like deep breathing, progressive muscle relaxation, and imagery *before* the triggering situation starts. If you can get through this difficult anticipatory period, your anxiety level will go down once you actually reach the feared situation (assuming no true danger exists).

You can also use your relaxation techniques regularly during the day, almost as a "reset" mechanism to counter the effects of sympathetic nervous system activation. As you encounter stressors throughout the day that activate your amygdala, you can keep downregulating it, much like your air-conditioning system turns on to cool your home.

This will help keep your stress level from building up as the day goes on. For example, consider a high school student going throughout her day. She experiences events that increase her stress, such as when teachers introduce confusing concepts, call on her in class, or mention an upcoming exam. If this student regularly practices deep breathing during the five-minute breaks she has between classes, she can reduce the accumulation of sympathetic nervous system activation that occurs during the day and send a message to her amygdala that school is not dangerous.

Ultimately, effective relaxation is an individualized process—how you relax depends on what works for you. We've focused on deep breathing, imagery, and progressive muscle relaxation; however, any method that activates the parasympathetic response can help, including massages, back scratches, and hot baths. Even humming, singing, or chanting can be effective because these activities activate the parasympathetic nervous system via the vagus nerve, which is connected to the vocal cords. Explore some different approaches to find what works best for you. Be sure to give them a fair try—don't just try something once and give up on it. Few of us have had training in how to counteract the effects of the amygdala, so it is a learning process, but you have the ability to take back control of your body.

Chapter 7

How Sleep Influences Your Amygdala

People often underestimate how essential sleep is. While they may believe it's important to sleep when they can, they don't believe they should make it a priority over other activities. But getting healthy sleep is crucial if you want a calm amygdala. When you get enough sleep, your amygdala is much less likely to have strong reactions to what you sense and experience. For example, research has found that when someone is limited to three hours of sleep for two days, they report higher levels of anxiety, and the connections between their amygdala and prefrontal cortex (a part of the brain that helps us deal with emotions) become weaker (Motomura et al., 2017). Even one night of sleep deprivation can make the amygdala react more strongly (Yoo et al., 2007). In fact, my clients who experience panic attacks often report having had poor sleep during the night (or nights) before the panic attack occurred. Therefore, if you are trying to tame your amygdala, getting healthy sleep is one of the most effective ways to do so.

Unfortunately, however, the amygdala itself often contributes to our sleep difficulties. When the amygdala is activated, it produces arousal in the brain that causes us to become alert and wakeful, which obviously makes sleep less likely. This explains why people who frequently experience anxiety, or who have an overactive amygdala, have difficulties falling asleep or getting back to sleep once awakened. This makes it difficult to get restful, extended sleep.

If you think about this, it makes perfect sense. Remember that we are the descendants of the frightened people. Our ancestors who survived and passed their genes on to us were likely to be those who took defensive actions to protect themselves and their children. They were more likely to survive if the amygdala kept them awake at night so they could defend against potential dangers, like a bear they had seen earlier in the day or a child who was sick with a fever. Because we descended from these individuals, *many of us also have an amygdala that keeps us awake if we are thinking about dangers*, even though the dangers of the modern world may be difficulties with paying our bills or an upcoming meeting at work.

Even if there is no immediate danger, and you are simply thinking about a distressing situation, this is enough to provoke the amygdala to produce arousal in the brain that interferes with your sleep. While you are trying to go to sleep, if you are thinking about stressful events that occurred earlier in the day or anticipating difficulties you may encounter tomorrow, the amygdala will react to these thoughts. Even though staying awake at night does not protect us from the kind of dangers we are thinking about, the amygdala still keeps us up because it is trying to defend us against all kinds of threats.

So we have a problem: Poor sleep gives us an activated amygdala, and having an activated amygdala makes it more difficult to get good sleep. It's a vicious cycle—but fortunately, there is a way out! This chapter will explain what kind of sleep you need and show you how you can achieve healthy sleep in spite of your amygdala.

What Kind of Sleep Keeps the Amygdala Calm?

When we sleep, we go through different stages, and a certain stage of sleep is particularly important for the amygdala. Multiple studies have shown that the amygdala is more likely to become activated if a person does not get enough rapid eye movement (REM) sleep (Altena et al., 2016; Motomura et al., 2017; Prather et al., 2013). During REM sleep, we experience dreams and our eyes move rapidly under our eyelids. In addition, the amygdala (among other brain regions) is active during REM sleep (Altena et al., 2016), and although we don't know the reason for it, the brain processes that occur during REM sleep are associated with a reduction in amygdala activation the next day (van der Helm et al., 2011).

In our **sleep architecture**, which is the pattern of sleep that we go through each night, REM sleep occurs only after we have cycled through the other stages. The pattern cycles from the lightest stage of sleep down to the stage right before REM, back up again, and then, finally, all the way down into REM sleep (figure 6). Our first period of REM sleep doesn't occur until we have been asleep for about 60 to 90 minutes, and it only lasts one to five minutes before the cycle moves on. Periods of REM sleep get longer as the night goes on and also occur more frequently, with the longest REM periods occurring in the last third of the night (Carskadon & Dement, 2011).

This means that to get healthy sleep for your amygdala, you need to sleep enough consecutive hours to reach the best REM phases. The National Sleep Foundation recommends that most adults sleep for seven to nine hours (Hirshkowitz et al., 2015), but you'll obtain more REM sleep if you sleep eight hours or more, since more REM sleep occurs in the last hours of sleep. If your sleep period isn't long enough, you are likely to get too little REM sleep, resulting in amygdala activation (Motomura et al., 2017; Prather et al., 2013). In contrast, if you sleep longer hours, you should notice that anxiety and panic are less likely to occur. Deliberately seeking sufficient sleep is beneficial for anyone dealing with anxiety.

Two important notes: First, the sleep period needs to be *uninterrupted* to be effective. When you wake up for 10 minutes or more, you can't always pick up where you left off in your sleep cycle (Grözinger et al., 2002). Getting back to sleep within 10 minutes can allow you to re-enter the sleep stage you were in when you woke up, but anything longer than that will start the sleep cycle over at the beginning—meaning it will take another 90 minutes to get back into one to five minutes of REM sleep. Therefore, avoid getting up in the night for prolonged periods, although a brief trip to the bathroom is not a problem.

Second, don't assume that napping is helpful for your amygdala. It is unlikely to provide any REM sleep, and it will often interfere with your ability to fall asleep later in the evening, shortening your hours of sleep.

Figure 6

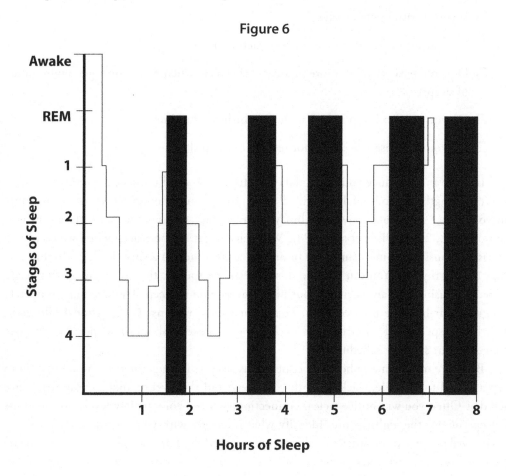

Healthy Sleep Checklists

Complete the following checklists to examine whether you are getting good sleep and, if not, to determine what is getting in the way. These checklists are based on research about what promotes good sleep and effective treatments for insomnia. Put a check mark next to any question that you would answer with a yes. If you mark any items in a particular list, make sure you read the section that follows that list for information and suggestions that will improve your sleep. By taking time to identify and remove barriers to healthy sleep, or to follow guidance on what promotes healthy sleep, you are more likely to be successful at obtaining the kind of sleep you need to calm your amygdala.

Do You Fail to Get Consistent, Lengthy Periods of Good Sleep?

❒ In a typical night, do you get less than eight hours of sleep?

❒ Is your bedtime inconsistent?

❒ Do you get up at inconsistent times each morning?

❒ Do you have two or more nights each week when you don't get eight hours of sleep?

❒ Do you tend to jump in bed without a bedtime routine?

❒ Do you feel unsatisfied and not rested after you sleep?

If you want to reduce your amygdala activation, you need to make a committed effort to obtain lengthy periods of REM-filled sleep. By getting enough REM sleep, not only can you reduce amygdala activation, but you can reduce the risk for panic attacks as well (Babson et al., 2009; Uhde et al., 1984). We typically get the best sleep when we go to bed and rise at consistent times, since our brains get accustomed to a specific sleep rhythm and adapt to that rhythm. You can achieve this by setting a specific time to begin getting ready for bed and using the same general routine before you go to sleep. Try to avoid completely changing your bedtime on weekends, except for special reasons. An occasional late night won't hurt, especially if you can sleep in, but every weekend should not mean a complete change in your sleeping schedule.

Be aware of how many hours of continuous sleep you are getting. It can be helpful to keep a record for a while, tracking both your sleep and the level of anxiety you experience each day. Often you will notice a clear connection between your anxiety level and the hours of sleep you got the night before. Identify what interferes with you getting ready for sleep, or what wakes you up, in order to adhere to your schedule. For example, if you stay up late to see a show or movie, next time consider recording it to watch at another time. If you get texts, phone calls, or alerts that delay your bedtime or interrupt your sleep, turn your phone off at a certain time. If you know you need to get up earlier than usual on a certain morning, begin your preparations for bedtime early so you still get sufficient sleep. These efforts can pay off in a calmer amygdala.

Do Activities in Your Daily Life Interfere with Good Sleep?

❒ Do you frequently take naps to help you get enough sleep?

❒ Does your work schedule interfere with your ability to get the sleep you want?

❒ Do you bring home your work and do it at night?

❒ Do you use your bedroom (especially your bed) to do work?

❒ Do your family and pet responsibilities interfere with your sleep?

Although you may not realize it, simple activities in your daily life may be interfering with your sleep. Being committed to a lengthy period of good sleep often requires that you take a careful look at what you do during the day. For example, napping can interfere with your ability to fall asleep, so with the exception of power naps (10–20 minutes), you should avoid napping, especially after 4 p.m.

Your work responsibilities may also affect your sleep and wake times. Obviously, it's not always possible to change your work circumstances, but you should recognize when work is compromising your sleep and consider whether you can take any steps to change that. Don't rule out asking your employer for a change in your schedule. Think creatively about ways to protect your sleep and make suggestions. Working from home has become more common in recent years, and you may find more flexibility than you expect, especially if it improves your productivity. In some cases, though, working from home may make it more difficult to step away from your job responsibilities—or, conversely, you may have caregiving responsibilities or distractions at home that make it difficult to complete your work on time. It can help to schedule specific "clock in" and "clock out" times so you can set good work-home boundaries and get yourself into bed in time for sufficient sleep.

In addition, doing work in bed can interfere with good sleep because your brain learns to associate your bed with work. In turn, your brain has a harder time "shutting off," which makes it more difficult to fall asleep. Therefore, make sure to use your bed only for sleep (and sexual activity), and avoid working and studying in your bed. In fact, when you have difficulty falling asleep, you shouldn't stay in bed awake for hours—you want your brain to associate the bed with sleeping, not with staying awake. If you can't sleep after 30 minutes or so, get out of bed and do something relaxing in dim light until you feel you can try to fall asleep again.

Family and pet responsibilities can also interfere with sleep, ranging from newborns who awaken multiple times per night to family pets that are a frequent source of early morning awakenings. To keep your amygdala calm, consider any reasonable methods to protect your sleep schedule, such as sharing responsibilities for childcare, carefully scheduling activities with pets or children, and training pets to follow your sleep habits rather than their own. Often, people don't take their need for sleep seriously and never even consider asking family members or employers to make accommodations, missing opportunities to have a calmer amygdala.

Of course, sometimes it's not feasible to make certain changes that would improve your sleep. The parent of a newborn can't simply ignore the baby's needs during the night, and some jobs require working long hours. Hopefully, the life circumstances that limit your sleep are temporary, and you don't give up your commitment to healthy sleep, especially if you see your anxiety worsening. Just remember to return to a healthy sleep schedule as soon as you can.

Do Your Diet and Exercise Habits Interfere with Good Sleep?

❏ Do you drink caffeine after 3 p.m.?

❏ Do you eat a large or spicy meal during the two or three hours before going to bed?

❏ Do you drink alcohol to help you fall asleep?

❏ Do you get little exercise?

❏ Do you exercise in the late evening?

What you eat and drink can impact your sleep quality, with caffeine in particular having significant effects. Caffeine interferes with sleep by increasing the amount of time it takes to fall asleep and reducing total sleep time (Roehrs & Roth, 2008). It also serves to activate both the amygdala (Smith et al., 2012) and the sympathetic nervous system (al'Absi & Lovallo, 2004), which increases levels of cortisol (a stress hormone) and blood pressure. People have different sensitivities to caffeine, so some react more strongly than others. In fact, some sensitivity to caffeine has been linked to certain genes that are also associated with being diagnosed with panic disorder (Childs et al., 2008). Even though people can develop a tolerance to caffeine, it still maintains the same activating effects on the sympathetic nervous system (al'Absi & Lovallo, 2004), so even regular caffeine drinkers can experience its negative effects. All these findings suggest that you should avoid consuming caffeine for six hours before going to bed (Drake et al., 2013) if you want your amygdala and your body to be ready for a good night's sleep.

Other types of food and drink can also interfere with sleep. While alcohol promotes relaxation and can get you to fall asleep faster, it also decreases sleep quality (Park et al., 2015), interferes with the brain's typical stages of sleep (Chan et al., 2013; Gourlay et al., 2016), and suppresses the amount of REM sleep early in the night (Van Reen et al., 2006). Therefore, it's not advisable to use alcohol as a sleep aid. In addition, eating spicy foods or consuming a very large meal before bed can cause indigestion and interfere with sleep.

Engaging in exercise during the day has been shown to improve sleep quality (Youngstedt & Kline, 2006), but the timing of exercise may matter. Engaging in physical activity within an hour of bedtime might make it difficult to fall asleep and shorten the length of sleep (Stutz et al., 2019), although some researchers have found this might not be a problem after all (Myllymäki et al., 2011). Therefore, if you find it convenient to exercise in the evening, you will need to determine whether late exercise helps you fall asleep or makes it more difficult.

Does Your Sleeping Environment Interfere with Good Sleep?

❏ Is your bed uncomfortable or too small?

❏ Do you often watch television, work on a computer, or look at your phone in bed?

❏ Is your bedroom too bright, too warm, too cold, or too noisy to allow you to sleep?

❐ Do you use an electric blanket to keep yourself warm?

❐ Do you often wake up and have difficulty getting back to sleep due to something in your environment?

❐ Does your sleeping partner make movements or sounds or have equipment that can interrupt your sleep?

❐ Do your children or pets sleep in the same bed as you?

In order to get good sleep, you need a bed that is comfortable and fits your needs, as well as a cool, quiet environment. The best room temperature for sleep is around 65 degrees (Pacheco, 2021) because your core body temperature needs to decrease during the night. In fact, difficulties with both falling asleep and early awakening have been linked with increased body core temperatures (Lack et al., 2008). Although skin warming (e.g., a hot bath) can help a person fall asleep, the body needs to cool in order for proper sleep cycling to occur (Harding et al., 2019). Heat (especially humid heat) has been shown to interfere with sleep (Okamoto-Mizuno & Mizuno, 2012), so using an electric blanket that remains on through the night may increase core body temperature and interfere with sleep (Raymann & van Someren, 2008). Feedback-controlled temperature regulation or the use of clothing, such as socks, to increase the temperature of specific body parts can allow the core body temperature to remain at an appropriate level for sleep.

In addition to temperature, light exposure is one of the strongest environmental influences on the human circadian rhythm (Chang et al., 2015). To be able to fall asleep readily, it helps to have good exposure to sunlight or bright light during the day and, just as importantly, to limit light exposure during the evening, something that doesn't always happen our modern lives. Not only do we have the ability to create continuously bright environments, but we are often tempted to binge-watch a show or scroll through our social media feed at night instead of winding down in preparation for sleep. Our brains rely on darkness to know when to release the right hormones to put us to sleep. Light—especially blue light, which is the type that's emitted by our digital devices—delays the release of the sleep-producing hormone, melatonin, making sleep more difficult (Chang et al., 2015). Light exposure in the evening also decreases REM time (Wams et al., 2017).

It is important to have a bedtime routine that allows you to prepare the brain for sleep. This can involve turning down the thermostat, dimming the lights, turning off electronic devices, and engaging in more relaxing activities, like reading a book. Even the simple activities you do already—like putting on your pajamas, washing your face, and brushing your teeth—can help train your brain to know that sleep is coming if you maintain a consistent routine. In fact, I have to be careful not to brush my teeth after 8 p.m. or I begin to feel tired because my brain associates brushing my teeth at night with falling asleep. Remember the importance of blue light in particular, and avoid screen time for at least one hour before bed, although it is acceptable to *listen* to your television, computer, or phone without extended eye contact with the screen.

Once you get in bed, it can be difficult to get quality sleep if you have pets or children who share the bed with you. You should weigh the importance of sleep when you respond to your pet's needs and train them in a way that protects your sleep. You should also consider making arrangements for children to sleep in their own beds, even though the transition may take some time. This extends to adult sleeping partners as well. If there's an aspect of your partner's sleep that interferes with yours—perhaps they snore, use a CPAP machine, or toss and turn all night—you might consider sleeping in separate rooms. Your relationship may improve from the benefits of reduced anxiety, and uninterrupted sleep plays a key role in this, so you should discuss options with your partner. Remember, if you get up for even 15 minutes, you may need to start your sleep cycle all over, which can significantly impact your amygdala—and your quality of life—for the next day or two.

Do Your Thoughts or Arousal Level Interfere with Sleep?

❒ Do you have difficulties falling asleep?

❒ Do you tend to worry when you get in bed to sleep?

❒ Do you fall asleep in front of the television?

❒ Do you have trouble relaxing enough to fall asleep?

❒ Do you frequently awaken at night?

❒ Do you often wake up and have difficulty getting back to sleep due to your thoughts?

❒ Do you have nightmares, night terrors, or problems with sleepwalking or sleep talking?

❒ Do you awaken and get up earlier than you need to when you want to stay asleep?

A common reason that people answer yes to these questions is the amygdala. When we are anxious or worrying about something, the arousal the amygdala produces can keep us from falling asleep or awaken us too early—or it can cause us to have parasomnias (e.g., night terrors, sleepwalking). While this may have kept our ancestors from being eaten by roaming tigers, in the modern world there typically aren't benefits to staying vigilant all night. The best way to cope with the arousal produced by the amygdala is to use deep breathing and muscle relaxation, as you learned in chapter 6. If you relax yourself, you relax the amygdala, and sleep is much more likely.

But just focusing on reducing arousal is not always effective because thoughts can also be a problem. Oftentimes, when people are lying in bed, they find themselves experiencing a variety of worries or anxiety-provoking thoughts, which activate the amygdala. Therefore, if you get in bed and begin worrying about the next day, your finances, or anything of importance to you, you are activating your amygdala, which is likely to prevent sleep. This is the reason why people often have an easier time falling asleep in front of the television: Whatever they're watching distracts them from their worries.

Many people who have trouble sleeping try to empty their mind of thoughts, but it is the nature of the brain to produce thoughts. Therefore, when amygdala-activating thoughts are keeping you awake, a more effective strategy is to *replace* these thoughts with thoughts that are more neutral. Like you do when watching television, you can change the channel in your brain so you are focused on another topic. To do so, listen to a podcast, a guided meditation, or an audiobook on your phone, television, or iPad—as long as you minimize looking at the screen to avoid the blue light. The only other requirement is that you keep your attention focused on what you are hearing so your thoughts do not stray into amygdala-activating territory. You can find many guided meditation and other apps to help you sleep.

When looking for an app, keep in mind that listening to music is typically not as helpful as listening to someone speaking because music does not interrupt and replace your thoughts as well as words alone do. Consider how difficult it is to focus on your own thoughts when someone is talking to you. Just be cautious not to listen to anything that is too interesting or exciting, remembering that your goal is to fall asleep. For example, you could listen to the same book on repeat since the goal is to focus your mind on something neutral, not necessarily to learn or experience anything new. This technique not only helps you fall asleep quickly, but it also helps you return to sleep if you tend to awaken in the night or too early in the morning. It can also help you fall back asleep after a nightmare because it gives you something else to focus on instead of the bad dream.

When we're under stress or have an upcoming event that may be distressing, it is perfectly natural to worry. But it doesn't help to lose sleep by focusing on these concerns in bed, so use these thought-replacing techniques to get to sleep as soon as you can. If you feel compelled to take some time to worry, do it during the daytime—at a time you specifically schedule for worrying—rather than during the hours when you need your sleep. Whenever you find yourself worrying outside of your scheduled worry time, make a mental note of it and table your worries until the scheduled worry time. In chapter 13, we'll talk more about how to do this.

What About Sleep Aids?

Although some medications can improve sleep, you should use these sparingly (National Institutes of Health, 2011). They typically are not intended for long-term use because of their negative side effects and decreasing effectiveness with regular use (Suni, 2020). Certain sleep aids are also riskier than others. Benzodiazepines, like alprazolam (Xanax) and clonazepam (Klonopin), and "Z-drug" hypnotics, like zaleplon (Sonata), zolpidem (Ambien), and eszopiclone (Lunesta), have a relaxing, sedating effect on the amygdala, but they can cause many negative side effects with regular, continued use, including insomnia, increased anxiety, and depression. They are considered high-risk drugs for elderly people in particular because they affect balance, can worsen cognitive impairment, and increase the risk of dementia (Kaiser Permanente, 2019; *Physicians' Desk Reference*, 2016). Therefore, it is important to consider their use only under the careful supervision of a physician. Naturally occurring hormones (like melatonin) and nonprescription medications (like diphenhydramine, the active ingredient in Benadryl) pose less risk than benzodiazepines or

Z-drugs, but you should still consult with your doctor before trying sleep aids, even those that are over-the-counter.

Given the risks of sleep aids, I recommend seeking more effective and lasting approaches to sleep difficulties, such as cognitive behavioral therapy for insomnia (CBT-I), which has demonstrated effectiveness in treating insomnia (Trauer et al., 2015) whether it is delivered by a therapist, as a self-help intervention, via interactive internet programs, or via email (Trockel et al., 2011). Many of the sleep hygiene and sleep environment recommendations discussed in this chapter are based on CBT-I principles. Relaxation and deep breathing are also commonly used. Many sleep difficulties can be effectively resolved by CBT-I, which incorporates additional, more involved interventions not addressed in this chapter, including biofeedback and sleep restriction (i.e., the use of sleep deprivation to promote sleep).

Getting Healthy Sleep

After examining your responses to the brief surveys in this chapter, you probably recognize that some of your habits and life circumstances are preventing you from giving your amygdala the sleep it needs, and as a result, it could become more activated, making you anxious, wary, jumpy, irritable, and even panicky. Hopefully, the information in this chapter has helped you understand what is happening in your brain so you can recognize that your feelings don't necessarily reflect an increased danger in your life—they simply reflect an amygdala that has not gotten enough sleep.

The following is a summary of the healthy sleep guidelines we've discussed. These guidelines are based on current research and evidence-based CBT-I approaches to insomnia, and they are designed to help you make the necessary changes to increase your REM sleep. Although it may not be possible to accomplish all the recommended steps in this list, the more you can accomplish, the more likely you will get the type of sleep you need to tame your amygdala.

Guidelines for Healthy Sleep Habits

- Go to bed early enough to get eight hours of uninterrupted sleep.

- Establish consistent sleep and wake times.

- Avoid napping except for 10-to-20-minute power naps.

- Refrain from doing work or other activities in bed (aside from sex) so your bed becomes associated primarily with sleeping.

- Limit caffeine intake, and stop drinking caffeinated beverages after 3 p.m.

- Don't use alcohol as a sleep aid.

- Refrain from eating large meals or spicy foods two to three hours before bedtime.

- Exercise for at least 30 minutes during the day at least three times per week.

- Don't engage in vigorous exercise in the hour before sleep; yoga is fine.

- Make your sleeping environment conducive to sleep. This includes:

  - Having a quiet, dark, and cool room

  - Having a comfortable, supportive bed

  - Not sleeping with children, pets, or partners who interfere with your sleep

  - Avoiding screen time while in bed

- Get sufficient exposure to bright lights and sunlight during the day.

- Reduce light exposure in the hours before bed, and avoid screen time for at least one hour before bed.

- Dim the lights and engage in a regular nightly ritual before going to bed each night to train your brain to expect sleep.

- Use muscle relaxation and breathing techniques in bed to prepare for sleep.

- If worries or anxious thoughts interfere with your ability to fall asleep, listen to audiobooks, podcasts, or guided meditations to replace those thoughts with neutral ones, remembering to limit light exposure from the screen.

- If you can't fall asleep after 30 minutes, get up and do something relaxing in a low-light environment until you feel sleepy, and then try to go to bed again.

- Avoid using sleep aids if possible, and limit their use if they are prescribed.

Even if you can only follow these guidelines for part of your week, you will probably find that your amygdala is less likely to produce the defense response or panic attacks. You may also find it helpful to keep track of how much uninterrupted sleep you get each night so you can see if you are reaching the target of eight hours or more. If you are keeping a Record of Daily Anxiety (from chapter 1), you can add it there to see if there's a relationship between your anxiety level and the hours of uninterrupted sleep you got the night (or nights) before. Record interrupted sleep as separate hours (like 4 + 3, instead of 7) because the longest periods of REM sleep occur after 4 or 5 hours of continuous sleep. Hopefully, as you get more opportunities for REM sleep, you'll have less anxiety!

Chapter 8

How Exercise and Diet Can Affect Your Amygdala

How Does Exercise Influence Your Amygdala?

So far, you have learned that when your amygdala activates the defense response, many of the changes in your body prepare you for the exertion needed to fight or flee. In other words, the amygdala prepares you to exercise your muscles. It is therefore not surprising that when you engage in physical activity, it has the effect of calming the amygdala. It is as if you have done what the amygdala thinks is necessary, so it stops creating the defense response. In fact, when I am feeling the defense response in my body, I often think to myself, "My amygdala wants me to run away," so I do some form of exercise, using my muscles in a way I believe will satisfy my amygdala.

When you are stressed or anxious, exercise can be effective at managing your amygdala in two specific ways: First, engaging in some form of aerobic exercise, especially if it uses the muscles in your arms and legs, takes advantage of the preparations that your amygdala has made for such an activity. The defense response initiates the release of adrenaline, increases the tension in your muscles, and routes blood flow to your arms and legs, so you might as well let your body do what it is prepared to do. For example, a friend of mine has a tendency to become anxious while driving, so he's learned to stop his car at a rest stop and jog around for 10 minutes or so. His teenage daughter rolls her eyes at him, but when he gets back in the car, he feels like his anxiety has washed away. Even though exercise is not likely to resolve the situation that led to your anxiety in the first place, it is still likely to reduce your anxiety because your amygdala only has a limited repertoire of responses (i.e., fight, flee, or freeze) when it tries to protect you from some potential danger.

Second, dozens of studies have shown that engaging in physical activity on a regular basis can reduce your general level of anxiety and lower depression as well (Bernstein et al., 2019; Ensari et al., 2015; Rebar et al., 2015). Therefore, if you are not in the habit of exercising regularly, you should consider doing so. Some of the effects of regular exercise relate directly to the defense response. For example, exercise affects the functioning of the sympathetic nervous system and the hypothalamic-pituitary-adrenal (HPA) axis, which makes activation of the defense response less likely (Anderson & Shivakumar, 2013). You may recall that the sympathetic nervous system and the hypothalamus are key players in producing the defense response, so when you find a way to reduce the defense response, you are targeting the root of anxiety.

Regular exercise also appears to cause changes in the amygdala that make activation less likely. For example, studies have shown that exercise can lead to new neural growth and can strengthen connections between the amygdala and other parts of the brain that keep the amygdala calmer (Anderson & Shivakumar, 2013; Chen et al., 2019). In addition, animal studies have shown that when rats are given the opportunity to run on a wheel in their cages, it promotes changes in neurons that use serotonin in the amygdala, which reduces the defense response (Leem et al., 2019). If you begin a regular exercise program, similar changes are likely to occur in your amygdala that make it less likely to become activated.

Any kind of aerobic exercise (the kind that increases your breathing and heart rate) will result in this effect. The following **Exercise Interest Inventory** provides you with a variety of exercises to choose from. But before you start an exercise program, you should consider your age and current health status. Some conditions—like an injury, diabetes, arthritis, or problems with your heart or breathing—may prevent you from being able to perform certain exercises. You may be limited to a certain type of exercise, like walking or gentle water aerobics, or you may need to use methods other than exercise to affect your amygdala. Consult with your physician if you have any concerns about beginning to increase your exercise. And don't overestimate what is required; simply walking for 30 minutes can be an effective aerobic exercise.

I can't tell you how many of my clients have reduced their general anxiety level and decreased the frequency of their panic attacks by incorporating regular exercise into their lives! Research has shown that consistent exercise can even lead to some of the same types of changes in the brain that serotonin reuptake inhibitors (SSRIs) or serotonin and norepinephrine reuptake inhibitors (SNRIs) do (Greenwood et al., 2012). For example, individuals have been shown to exhibit neural growth (i.e., neurogenesis) in the amygdala, hippocampus, and cortex after using SSRIs and SNRIs, as well as after engaging in regular exercise (Anderson & Shivakumar, 2013). In some cases, my clients have had periods of time when they wanted to wean off medications, perhaps because of a pregnancy or to determine whether the medication was still needed. By participating in a regular exercise program, they were able to safely and more smoothly transition (under a physician's supervision) to a period of life without medication.

Exercise Interest Inventory

For your amygdala to reap the benefits of regular exercise, you must exercise routinely, meaning that it should involve at least 30 minutes of activity three to five times per week. To make this easier to achieve, you should choose activities that you have sufficient interest in so you can stay motivated to engage in exercise on a regular basis. The following is a list of activities that, if done regularly, can give you the kind of aerobic exercise that will provide you with a generally calmer amygdala. Rate your interest in each activity using a scale of 1 to 5, with 1 being "little interest" and 5 being "a great deal of interest."

_____ Basketball   _____ Raking leaves

_____ Biking   _____ Rowing

_____ Canoeing   _____ Shoveling snow

_____ Cardio drumming   _____ Skating (roller, inline, ice)

_____ Climbing stairs   _____ Soccer

_____ Cross-country skiing   _____ Stationary bicycle

_____ Elliptical machine   _____ Swimming

_____ Dance video workout   _____ Tennis

_____ Dancing   _____ Treadmill

_____ Jazzercise   _____ Video-based workouts

_____ Jogging or running   _____ Volleyball

_____ Jumping jacks   _____ Walking a dog

_____ Jump rope   _____ Walking in water

_____ Kayaking   _____ Walking or hiking

_____ Kickboxing   _____ Water aerobics

_____ Pushing a lawnmower   _____ Zumba

After considering all of these potential activities, can you select one or more to provide yourself with regular aerobic exercise? You needn't always engage in the same activity. You can include a variety of activities in your schedule, as long as it gives you an opportunity for 30 minutes of aerobic exercise, three to five times a week. This will typically allow you to see a difference in your anxiety level. Start slowly and work your way up to longer and more frequent periods of exercise. You may also want to ask a friend or family member to join you because having a partner can increase your commitment to maintaining a regular exercise routine.

In addition, don't forget that exercise can be used on an *as-needed* basis to cope with anxiety or panic. That's because aerobic exercise is one of the best ways to reduce activation in the amygdala fairly quickly. For example, a teenage client of mine who struggled with social anxiety was very anxious and uncomfortable about the annual family reunion that was being held at her home. But after she left the reunion and jogged around her neighborhood for a while, she found that she suddenly felt much calmer and was able to speak comfortably to her aunts, uncles, and cousins. She was so impressed by the way her amygdala responded to exercise in that specific situation that she was motivated to use jogging as a coping strategy for other situations, such as an upcoming exam or an argument with a friend.

Engaging in aerobic exercise for even 10 or 15 minutes can be very helpful when you are anxious. Even if it is just going for a brisk walk or turning on some music you can dance to, you can calm your amygdala down by activating your body's large muscle groups through exercise. Engaging in physical activity can also improve your sleep, increase alertness and concentration, and reduce cholesterol and blood pressure. The positive changes that can result from exercise are remarkable.

How Does Your Diet Influence Your Amygdala?

Did you know that what you eat and drink can also affect your amygdala? Although most people are aware of the connection between caffeine and anxiety, many do not realize that sugar can also have an impact on anxiety. Therefore, it's important to take a close look at your eating and drinking habits to make sure you are maintaining a diet that keeps you calm instead of increasing stress in your body.

Caffeine

Caffeine—the most popular drug in the world (Rogers, 2007)—has been shown to increase feelings of anxiety by activating the sympathetic nervous system and initiating the release of adrenaline, just like the defense response (Brice & Smith, 2002; Rogers et al., 2006; Veleber & Templer, 1984). While some of us can handle caffeine without difficulty, people who already experience high levels of amygdala activation may find that caffeine causes too much additional nervous system stimulation, resulting in unwanted increases in blood pressure and heart rate.

Caffeine sensitivity varies from person to person and seems to be influenced by genetics (Childs et al., 2008). To assess the extent to which you are sensitive to caffeine, you need to know where caffeine is appearing in your diet and what dosage you are getting. Most people are aware that caffeine is in coffee, tea, energy drinks, and many soft drinks. But the amount of caffeine in these drinks can vary greatly, with drip and percolated coffee having almost twice the caffeine of instant coffee, and many caffeinated teas having only half the caffeine of coffee. You may also be surprised to realize that the caffeine level in coffee varies from brand to brand and also that caffeine is present in chocolate! You can find detailed information online about different sources of caffeine and the amount of caffeine in each. (See the Center for Science in the Public Interest for a useful table: https://www.cspinet.org/eating-healthy/ingredients-of-concern/caffeine-chart.)

Anytime you are wondering why your anxiety spiked or why you had a panic attack, don't forget to consider whether caffeine intake contributed to the defense response you experienced. Although people who are sensitive to caffeine are usually very aware of this reality, some are completely unaware that a seemingly innocent cup of coffee can impact their anxiety. For example, one of my clients returned for therapy after he had successfully learned to manage his OCD. He told me that his symptoms had come back after he got a new job, and he was once again having a great deal of difficulty resisting the desire to compulsively clean. As we discussed his new job, he reported that he had access to unlimited coffee in the office, so he had begun drinking a great deal of it. When I suggested that he cut out the coffee, he soon realized that it had been causing the increase in his symptoms. He called me and said, "I don't need another appointment. I cut out the coffee and feel back in control again."

However, if you have been regularly including caffeine in your diet, cutting it out without a gradual taper is likely to result in withdrawal symptoms, which can include headache, fatigue, low energy, muscle pain, poor concentration, irritability, and even anxiety. These symptoms will subside as your brain adjusts to the absence of caffeine, usually within two to seven days. If you decide to completely remove caffeine from your diet, it might help to substitute a similar food or drink—for example, replacing your usual cup of coffee with a noncaffeinated herbal tea—so you still have the comfort of that routine.

Alternatively, you may find it unnecessary to completely cut caffeine out of your diet and choose to simply reduce your caffeine intake or limit the times when you ingest it. But don't forget—caffeine interferes with both the feeling of tiredness and the regular sleep cycle, and good sleep is essential in regulating the amygdala's functioning. Many people report that caffeine doesn't interfere with their ability to fall asleep, but this doesn't mean that their sleep is unaffected. Research has shown that those who ingest caffeine have less sleep time and poorer sleep quality, as evidenced by decreases in stages 3 and 4 of sleep and suppressed EEG slow-wave activity (Roehrs & Roth, 2008; Watson et al., 2016). Caffeine remains in the body for six hours after it is ingested, so it can easily still be present in the brain when you retire to bed if you ate or drank it in the afternoon (Drake et al., 2013). Make sure not to ingest caffeine for at least six hours before going to bed to decrease its negative effects on your sleep.

Sugar

The amount of sugar in your diet is another important factor that can affect your amygdala. If you eat irregularly—going for long periods without food and then eating a great deal when you have the opportunity—you are going to have large fluctuations in your blood sugar (glucose) level. These swings will definitely get your amygdala's attention. That's because the amygdala has glucose-sensing regions that monitor blood sugar levels (Zhou et al., 2010), so it knows when you experience low glucose levels even if *you* don't. Animal studies have shown that during periods of low glucose levels, the amygdala reacts with increased activation, producing heightened anxiety (McNay, 2015). Therefore, to keep your amygdala from reacting, a stable level of blood sugar throughout the day is recommended.

For many people, paying attention to their own glucose levels is essential knowledge in taming the amygdala. Glucose is the fuel for our cells, especially our brain cells, which use more fuel than any other organ in the human body, so the amygdala interprets the absence of glucose as a clear and present danger. Just like the low fuel light in your car lets you know when your gas tank is almost empty, the amygdala reacts to alert you to the potentially dire situation of low fuel in your brain. Low blood sugar (which is called *hypoglycemia*) can occur for a variety of reasons—such as skipping meals, eating less than normal, or having diabetes—and some people are more sensitive to hypoglycemia than others. The following checklist presents many common symptoms of hypoglycemia.

Symptoms of Hypoglycemia

Consider how you feel when you (1) go three or four hours after a meal without eating anything, (2) wake up in the morning and have not yet had breakfast, or (3) eat or drink a very sweet food or beverage and follow it with no other food for over an hour. If you experience any of the symptoms below, it may be due to the effects of hypoglycemia. Put a check mark by any symptoms you experience in these kinds of situations.

- ❑ Irritability
- ❑ Headache
- ❑ Feeling overwhelmed
- ❑ Fatigue
- ❑ Hunger
- ❑ Lightheadedness
- ❑ Jumpiness
- ❑ Moodiness
- ❑ Craving for sweets, carbs, or alcohol
- ❑ Racing or uneven heart rate
- ❑ Shakiness or trembling
- ❑ Confusion
- ❑ Difficulty concentrating
- ❑ Weakness
- ❑ Impaired coordination
- ❑ Panic

You can see that many of these symptoms are very similar to what we feel in other cases of amygdala activation. This is not surprising because adrenaline is released when a person experiences hypoglycemia (McNay, 2015), both as a result of the body's general reaction to low blood sugar and due to any reaction from the amygdala. When hypoglycemia is the cause of these symptoms, they will fade if we simply eat or drink something that increases our blood sugar, such as fruit juice or some hard candy. However, it's best that our bodies have a steady fuel supply so we can avoid experiencing low blood glucose levels, as it can take the brain an hour to return to normal functioning following hypoglycemia (Sircar et al., 2016).

While we all suffer from hypoglycemia from time to time, some of us are more prone to it as a result of our diet, eating schedule, exercise routine, or other physiological factors. Your doctor can order a simple test to determine whether you are prone to hypoglycemia and, if so, you can make certain lifestyle modifications to maintain a stable blood sugar level and avoid experiencing this problem. For example, it's important to eat regularly during the day so you don't go long periods of time without replenishing the fuel supply needed to support activities in your body and your brain. In addition, before exercising, make sure to eat foods that make glucose available to your muscles so your exertion does not cause hypoglycemia. Foods such as beans, whole grain bread, and pasta should be eaten two to three hours before a workout, while fruits should be eaten just before. Your body—especially your brain—needs energy from glucose and other sugars.

When examining your own diet, it's important to know that a variety of sugars—including white sugar, brown sugar, honey, molasses, fructose, and corn syrup—can affect the stability of blood glucose levels. Sweet foods and drinks result in a quick rise in blood sugar levels because the body processes and consumes the sugars in these foods very rapidly, but this is followed by a quick drop as the sugar is quickly utilized in our cells. When this quick rise and drop occurs, the amygdala reacts as if you were to detect a sudden decrease in the amount of gas in your car: "Oh, no!" Fructose, which is found in fruits and fruit juices, has this rapid effect on blood sugar, as do carbohydrates like potatoes, pasta, white bread, candies, and cookies.

However, not all carbohydrates are created equally. *Processed* carbohydrates—like white bread, pasta, white rice, sweetened cereals, cookies, chips, and pretzels—are utilized more quickly by the body, resulting in more spikes and drops in your blood sugar level. Unfortunately, processed carbohydrates have been stripped down to their most basic components and have little nutritional value, so you need to eat more foods to get the nutrients you need for the day. For example, in the process of making white flour, the bran and germ of the wheat is removed—along with 20 different nutrients. Even when flour is "enriched" to restore nutrients, only four nutrients are added back in (Bourne et al., 2004).

In contrast, *complex* carbohydrates provide you with fiber, vitamins, minerals, and nutrients, as well as a supply of glucose. This includes foods such as whole grain bread, brown rice, whole grain pasta, fresh fruits and vegetables, and various legumes. The body digests complex carbohydrates more slowly, which helps prevent sharp fluctuations in blood sugar, especially when the foods contain fiber to make them break down even more slowly. The *glycemic index* is a way to classify carbohydrates according to the extent to which they raise blood sugar, and it can be useful in selecting foods that will help you avoid hypoglycemia. Higher glycemic values reflect foods that lead to quicker increases in blood sugar (Atkinson et al., 2008). The table here provides the glycemic index for several common foods, though you can find this information for almost any food online.

Glycemic Index of Common Foods

Food	Glycemic Index	Food	Glycemic Index
White bread	75 ± 2	Apple juice	41 ± 2
Specialty grain bread	53 ± 2	Orange juice	50 ± 2
Corn tortilla	46 ± 4	Strawberry jam	49 ± 3
White rice, boiled	73 ± 4	Potato, boiled	78 ± 4
Brown rice, boiled	68 ± 4	French fries	75 ± 5
Sweet corn	53 ± 5	Sweet potato, boiled	63 ± 6
Spaghetti	49 ± 2	Carrots, boiled	39 ± 4
Couscous	65 ± 4	Ice cream	51 ± 3
Cornflakes	81 ± 6	Yogurt	41 ± 2
Instant oatmeal	79 ± 3	Kidney beans	24 ± 4
Apple	36 ± 2	Lentils	32 ± 5
Orange	43 ± 3	Popcorn	65 ± 5
Banana	51 ± 3	Potato chips	56 ± 3

You can also modify the impact of carbohydrates on blood glucose by combining them with other foods. Combining carbohydrates with proteins (like meat, fish, eggs, beans, nuts, or dairy products) and non-starchy vegetables (like carrots, cauliflower, mushrooms, spinach, or tomatoes) is helpful because it takes longer for your body to break down these foods. Eating a variety of foods with varying glycemic values will also result in a more gradual release of glucose that is sustained over time. I used to explain this to my children by telling them that eating certain foods was like lighting a single match that wouldn't provide light for very long. Other foods keep your energy burning for much longer, as if you had lit a candle. Choose foods that will keep your energy burning.

Although sugar substitutes may seem like a good idea, they are designed to produce a sweet taste in our mouth, which overstimulates sugar receptors and can change our palate preferences. This can increase sugar cravings rather than decrease them, and it may affect how we taste other foods. Artificial sweeteners have also been shown to block the production of the neurotransmitter serotonin and cause increased anxiety (Ashok et al., 2015). Therefore, instead of using sweeteners, we should work on decreasing our sugar consumption, saving it for special occasions. Ironically, when you ingest less sugar, your body stops craving it so much.

You may also be surprised to learn that alcohol consumption can strongly affect blood glucose levels. Many alcoholic drinks have a high sugar content, but even drinking unsweetened alcoholic beverages can result in hypoglycemia. That's because the processing of alcohol puts a great demand on the liver, which typically maintains stable blood sugar by producing glucose, so ingesting alcohol can prevent the liver from doing its job. Although people with anxiety often resort to alcohol because of its anxiety-reducing effects in the short term, they don't realize this will likely cause their blood sugar to rise as their liver focuses on processing alcohol and then fall rapidly after they stop drinking—which can then cause a resurgence of anxiety symptoms. These drops in blood sugar levels can last up to 12 hours after alcohol is consumed. Therefore, it's important to avoid the use of alcohol if you are trying to stabilize your blood sugar levels. The following checklist provides you with some additional guidelines to prevent hypoglycemia.

Guidelines for Maintaining a Stable Blood Sugar Level

1. If you feel that you are having a consistent problem with hypoglycemia, check with your physician, who can review your symptoms and conduct a physical exam, including an assessment of your blood sugar level. You may be advised to take a glucose tolerance test that assesses how your body responds to your blood sugar level. Your physician can best advise you whether you have a type of hypoglycemia that requires treatment.

2. Prevent spikes in your blood sugar level by eating foods with a high glycemic index in moderation.

3. Eat breakfast, including foods containing protein (e.g., yogurt, eggs, meat), soon after waking and before drinking coffee, because caffeine reduces your appetite when you need to refuel. Instead of eating processed carbohydrates like sweetened cereals, choose whole grains and oatmeal, which fuel your body longer.

4. Eat meals that include a variety of foods, including protein (meat, fish, eggs, beans, nuts, or dairy products) and high-fiber foods (whole grains and vegetables) so they digest more slowly.

5. Eat smaller meals and have snacks during the day so you are providing stable fuel for yourself about every three hours.

6. If you wake up late at night or early in the morning with symptoms of anxiety, consider whether hypoglycemia is playing a role. Have a snack containing complex carbohydrates or protein before going to bed or when you wake up to help prevent hypoglycemia.

Chapter 9

How Your Amygdala Creates Triggers

Up to this point, our focus has been on helping you better understand the amygdala and learn ways to manage how it functions. Although chapter 5 focused on the language of the amygdala, it didn't address one important aspect of communication: the language you need to learn so you can communicate *new* information to this part of your brain. Learning this language will allow you to teach your amygdala to respond differently.

The amygdala's ability to learn is what makes it so valuable to so many species of animals. The amygdala can learn to fear objects and situations as a means of protecting us from threats that didn't exist for previous generations or earlier in our lives. That is, it can adapt to the specific situation in which an animal lives. Consider a squirrel that has found a certain fenced-in yard filled with acorns. If the squirrel experiences a negative event in that yard, like being chased by a dog, then the squirrel's amygdala will learn to react to the yard as if it is dangerous. It will produce the defense response whenever the squirrel approaches the fenced yard, preparing the squirrel to fight, flee, or freeze. This learning is not about logic, and it does not require cause and effect. The squirrel simply experienced the fenced yard and the dog at the same time.

In the same way, when you experience a negative event, your amygdala is likely to identify situations or objects that coincided with that event as dangerous. That's because the amygdala is designed to learn from experience on the basis of *association*. When a certain location or object is associated (or paired) with a negative experience, the amygdala learns to respond to that location or object as dangerous by creating new neural connections in the brain associated with fear (Quirk et al., 1995).

Neurons, which are certain cells in the brain, form memories when two different neurons are activated at the same time (Hebb, 1949). You may have heard Carla Shatz's famous phrase "neurons that fire together wire together" (Doidge, 2007), which means that a memory is formed when a connection between neurons forms. In the case of the squirrel, two different sets of neurons began firing at the same time: the neurons that were processing the experience of being in the fenced-in yard and the neurons that were processing the experience of being chased by a dog. This caused the squirrel's amygdala to create neural circuitry—that is, to form an emotional memory—that associated the fenced-in yard with danger, causing the squirrel to respond with fear.

Understanding Triggers

In order to learn the language of the amygdala, it is important to understand how it creates *triggers*, which are things that your amygdala has come to associate with danger and that therefore evoke anxiety and other aspects of the defense response. In the previous example, the fenced-in yard became a trigger for the squirrel. A variety of objects, entities, locations, situations, and sensory stimuli can be triggers, depending on a person's experiences. Some people are triggered by crowded streets, classrooms, or buses, while others are triggered by certain sounds and smells. Although you may already be familiar with your own triggers, you may not have been aware that the amygdala is responsible for the anxiety you experience in response to these triggers. The following worksheet will help you better recognize and understand your triggers.

Identify Your Triggers

In the space below, list the situations that often cause anxiety when you encounter them. Include any locations, experiences, objects, people, animals, smells, sounds, and so on. Making this list of your own triggers will help you to understand and apply what you read throughout this chapter.

_____

_____

_____

_____

_____

_____

_____

_____

_____

_____

_____

_____

_____

_____

The amygdala creates a trigger when something has been associated with a negative event (figure 7). Association occurs when the trigger is experienced *just before or at the same time as* the negative event. A negative event is any situation that results in a person having a negative physical or emotional response, like pain, discomfort, embarrassment, or distress.

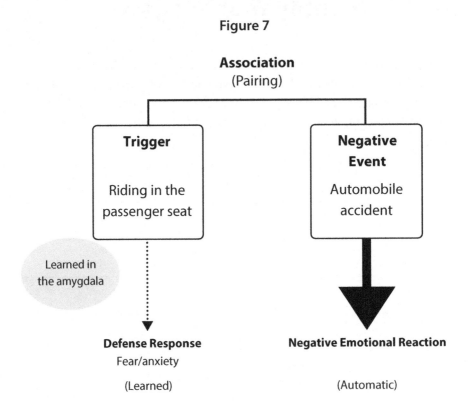

Figure 7

Association
(Pairing)

Trigger	**Negative Event**
Riding in the passenger seat	Automobile accident

Learned in the amygdala

Defense Response
Fear/anxiety

(Learned)

Negative Emotional Reaction

(Automatic)

For example, Jeremy was riding in Leo's car when another car collided with them. Leo's car was totaled, but luckily Jeremy and Leo had only minor injuries. Nevertheless, it was a very distressing event. Because Jeremy was riding in the passenger seat when the accident occurred, riding in the passenger seat (*trigger*) was paired (*associated*) with the accident (*negative event*). Even though he'd never had a problem riding in a car, after the accident Jeremy found that riding in the passenger seat of any car was now a trigger for the defense response, including anxiety. Jeremy was still able to drive a car without any problem; he only experienced anxiety when he tried to sit in the passenger seat.

Notice that the trigger does not need to be dangerous or cause the negative event to occur. The trigger is simply *associated with* the negative event. That's because when a negative event happens, the amygdala forms an emotional memory, creating neural circuits that connect the trigger with feelings of fear or anxiety. As a result, your brain becomes conditioned to activate the defense response when the trigger is present. The amygdala also creates positive emotional memories when something is associated with a pleasant event, such as the shoes you wore during your team's winning basketball season. Because of the positive events that occurred when you were wearing those shoes, you may feel positive emotions whenever you see them, and you may not be willing to part with them.

The emotional memories created by the amygdala are different from the conscious memories formed by the cortex. You may have triggers that don't seem to make sense because you don't remember ever having a negative experience involving that trigger. If so, the memory of the event is not stored in your cortex, but it certainly appears that your amygdala has retained a memory. This is possible because the amygdala forms memories in a completely separate way from the cortex. Your cortex creates the "story" memories you are aware of, but the amygdala forms the memories that underlie your emotional reactions. So your amygdala can still remember these triggers as dangerous, even if you do not remember why.

This process is well illustrated by a little "experiment" that a physician once carried out on one of his patients (Claparède, 1951). (Please note this is an experiment I would never approve of!) The patient had Korsakov's syndrome, a form of dementia in which a person loses the ability to make new memories in the cortex. Therefore, she could not remember the medical staff who cared for her day after day, even though she had lived in the hospital for years. Each time the physician came in, he had to introduce himself all over again because the patient was unable to form any memory of him. To test the patient's memory, one day the physician put his hand out to shake her hand, and he poked her with a pin he had concealed in his palm. On his next visit, when he approached the patient and put his hand out, she pulled back in fear. He asked her why she wouldn't shake his hand, and she said she didn't know. Although she didn't recall ever seeing the physician before, she would not agree to shake his hand. Her cortex did not remember him, but her amygdala certainly did.

Throughout your life, your amygdala has been making note of any object, location, person, or situation that has been associated with a negative event, particularly those that resulted in a negative emotional reaction. It has carefully stored in memory everything associated with that negative event—identifying it with an emotional tag—so that whenever you encounter that trigger again, your amygdala will cause you to experience anxiety or even a full-blown defense response. In addition, you can form multiple triggers in response to one negative event. For example, Jeremy, who was in the car accident described earlier, may react not only to sitting in the passenger seat, but also to the sound of brakes squealing or horns honking, if those were associated with the accident.

Your amygdala can even create triggers in response to negative events that you did not personally experience, but that you observed someone else experience. Let's say your mother exhibits an obvious fear of swimming. Your amygdala can also learn to fear water simply by observing her fear. You can imagine how useful it has been across the centuries for humans to learn to fear anything previously associated with bad things happening to you or others, as well as to identify something as dangerous if others react to it with fear. The amygdala is a powerful protector because it *learns from experience.* This is important to remember as you learn how to communicate with your amygdala.

Now that you understand how and why the amygdala creates triggers, you're ready to start looking more closely at your personal triggers. Remember, both the trigger and the negative event are real experiences that you can see, hear, feel, smell, or taste. The trigger differs from the negative event in that you *learn* to fear the trigger, whereas the negative event is something to which most people would *naturally* have a negative reaction.

Often, triggers result in emotions you know are not logical, and you recognize that most other people would not respond to the trigger the same way you do. By continuing in this workbook, you can learn more about your triggers—including how to reduce the effect they have on you.

Diagramming Triggers

One way to identify how your amygdala learned your triggers is to diagram them. In some cases, you may have a very clear memory of the negative event associated with the trigger. For example, you might feel anxious whenever you see a hornet because you remember receiving a painful sting when you were a child. In other cases, you may not remember what the negative event was, but you might be able to find out by asking other people in your life, such as your family members. For example, a Black woman who grew up in the Jim Crow era had the childhood experience of being rudely turned away from a segregated swimming pool while wearing her new red swimsuit. Both she and her mother felt humiliated by the experience. From that day on, the girl would never wear that swimsuit, and she even disliked wearing anything that was red. Although she later couldn't remember why, her mother could tell her the story of how the color red had become a trigger for her.

In the following worksheet, you'll have an opportunity to practice diagramming some hypothetical triggers, followed by some of your own triggers. Use the diagram in figure 8 as a guide.

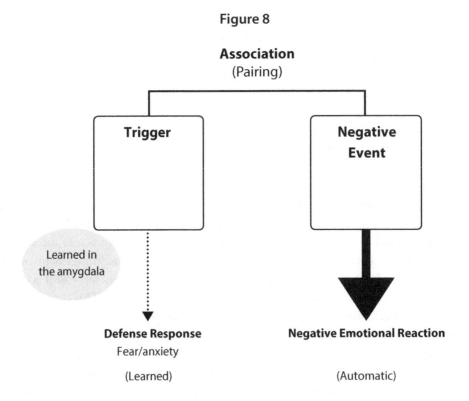

Figure 8

Association
(Pairing)

| Trigger | Negative Event |

Learned in the amygdala

Defense Response
Fear/anxiety

(Learned)

Negative Emotional Reaction

(Automatic)

Diagramming Triggers

Practice diagramming the three situations provided by identifying the **trigger** and the **negative event** for each. Use the template in figure 8 to help you sketch out your diagrams. Remember that the trigger does not need to be the cause of the negative event; it only needs to be associated with it. That's why some fears seem illogical, even to the people who have them.

The correct answers can be found at the end of this chapter.

1. After being sexually assaulted by a man with a shaved head, Rebecca has anxiety whenever she is around bald men.

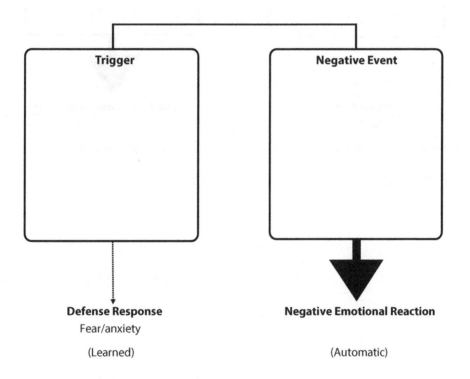

Trigger	Negative Event
Defense Response Fear/anxiety (Learned)	**Negative Emotional Reaction** (Automatic)

2. Jason was walking in the woods when a thunderstorm suddenly developed. A tree near him was struck by lightning, and it exploded with a deafening crash. Now Jason is uncomfortable walking in the woods.

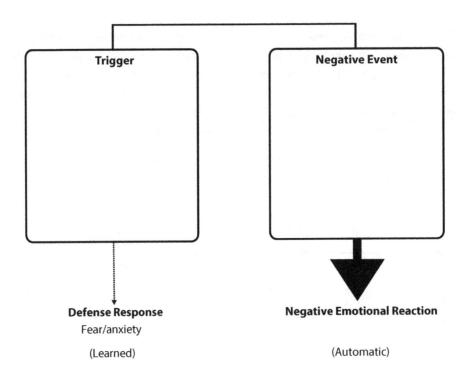

Trigger

Negative Event

Defense Response
Fear/anxiety

(Learned)

Negative Emotional Reaction

(Automatic)

3. Heather often sat in the front of her college classrooms because she felt it helped her pay attention. After one professor teased her about giving an incorrect answer, Heather began avoiding sitting in the front.

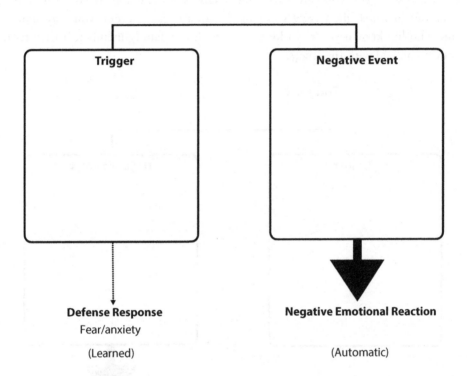

Trigger

Negative Event

Defense Response
Fear/anxiety

(Learned)

Negative Emotional Reaction

(Automatic)

Now that you have had some practice with these situations, you are ready to diagram your own triggers. Return to the list of triggers you created in the **Identify Your Triggers** worksheet. For each trigger, consider when you first began responding to the trigger with anxiety or avoidance. Can you remember a negative event that occurred right after or at the same time as the trigger? If so, try to diagram this association. By identifying the situation that created this trigger, you can better understand your reaction. If you can't remember any situations in which the trigger was paired with a negative event, you may want to ask someone who has known you for a long time, such as a family member, if they recall any experiences you had with the trigger.

Trigger 1: _____

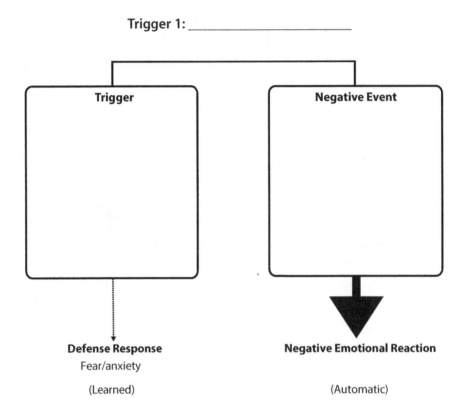

Trigger 2: _____

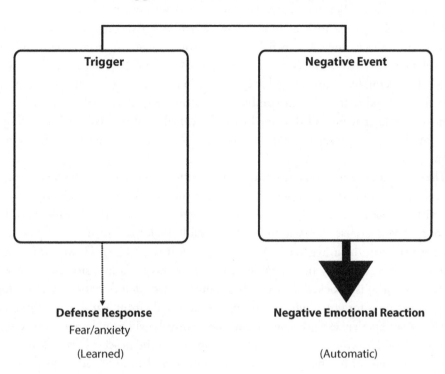

Defense Response
Fear/anxiety

(Learned)

Negative Emotional Reaction

(Automatic)

Trigger 3: _____

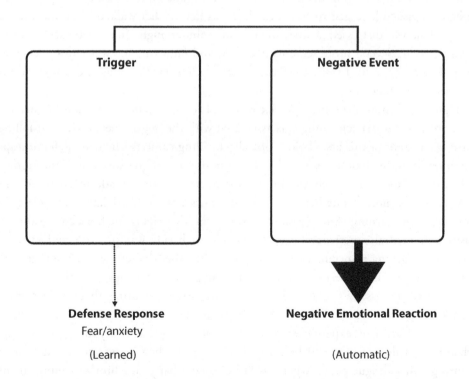

Defense Response
Fear/anxiety

(Learned)

Negative Emotional Reaction

(Automatic)

Learning the association-based language of the amygdala can help you to understand how your amygdala relies on past experiences to determine what objects or situations it identifies as dangerous in the present day. When you recognize why the amygdala is responding the way it does, it can help you see your triggers in a new light. Many fears that developed when we were children remain even though they don't really make sense anymore. For example, many of us have an aversion to hearing our full name because it was often associated with being in trouble: "Catherine Marie! What have you done?!" Bill Clinton once said that he still did not like to be called William. Isn't it interesting that a person could become president and still have his full name trigger a negative emotional reaction?

These negative emotional reactions will continue until the amygdala is presented with new information that changes the way it responds. Remember: A trigger must be paired with a negative event in order for the amygdala to learn to identify that object as dangerous. If you expose yourself to a trigger while making sure it is *not* paired with a negative experience, the amygdala can learn to *not* fear the trigger. However, people often live their lives in such a way that they never put their amygdala in a situation to learn. For example, a boy who is knocked down by his grandmother's dog develops a fear of dogs and keeps avoiding dogs for years, which prevents his amygdala from learning anything new. As long as no new experiences with dogs occur, the amygdala will not change its reaction.

In contrast, let's consider an example that illustrates the process of new learning in the amygdala. Jane fell off her horse when it got spooked and jumped sideways during a trail ride with her family. She rode back to the stable on her mother's horse, with her mother sitting right behind her. Jane's family continued to encourage her to ride with them on the trails, but she was afraid and unwilling to go. Finally, Jane's mom saddled the gentlest horse they had and asked Jane just to sit on the horse as her mother walked it around the stable. Although Jane was distressed at first, she became calm enough after several sessions to take the reins herself. Several more sessions like that, and Jane said she was willing to take this horse out onto the trails. Eventually, Jane's mom could even encourage her to try riding the horse that she had fallen off.

Figure 9 illustrates the process that was used to assist Jane in overcoming her fear of horses. For Jane, horseback riding was associated with the negative experience of falling off a horse. As a result of this association, horseback riding came to elicit the defense response in Jane, resulting in anxiety, fear, and a strong desire to flee the situation. Jane's amygdala had learned to identify horseback riding as dangerous, which made it a trigger for her. But when Jane's mother put her on the gentle horse, she offered Jane's amygdala a new opportunity for learning. She repeatedly paired the experience of horseback riding with a positive or neutral experience by ensuring that each ride was pleasant and safe, which allowed new learning to occur. Gradual exposure like this—where we ensure that nothing negative happens—is the best way to teach the amygdala that a trigger is safe.

As we've discussed, you may not know the original pairing that made something a trigger in the first place. But that's okay—you don't need to remember the negative experience to form new experiences that calm your amygdala. If a young boy is afraid of baseball bats, it doesn't matter if he formed this trigger when he was accidentally hit by a bat during a little league game, when his father used a bat to hit him as a punishment, or when a neighborhood bully threatened him with one. In each case, the best way to change his amygdala's response is to repeatedly expose him to baseball bats without anything negative occurring. Eventually, this will teach his amygdala to respond differently, which decreases amygdala activation as new memories are formed (Roy et al., 2014). This process, which is called exposure, will be the focus of the next chapter.

Figure 9

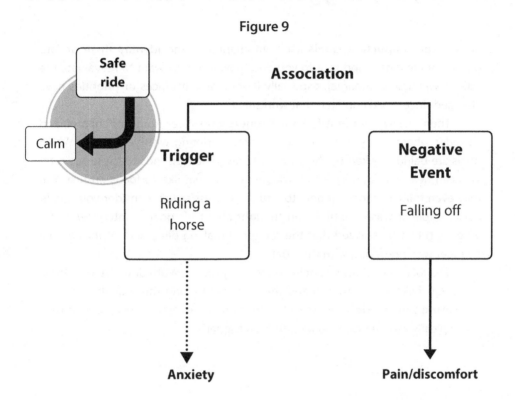

Identifying Triggers That Block Your Goals

Before moving on to the next chapter, I would like you to consider how your life would be different if your amygdala did not produce the defense response to certain triggers. What goals would you be able to accomplish? Use the following worksheet to help you identify the triggers that are preventing you from reaching your goals, since these are the triggers that you will want to work on overcoming first. For example, a landscape architect in Arizona may find that her fear of snakes is restricting her ability to conduct plant inventory when she surveys project sites. On the other hand, a fashion designer in New York City who also fears snakes may not have any need to reduce that fear because it doesn't interfere with her day-to-day life or career aspirations. You will want to focus on the triggers that keep you from accomplishing the goals you have set for yourself. By working to overcome these triggers, you are making a change in the amygdala, and that will make a difference in your life.

Identifying Triggers That Block Your Goals

Review your **Important Goals** list from chapter 3, and identify three or four goals that are most important to you right now. You may want to reevaluate the ratings you assigned earlier, especially if your circumstances or priorities have changed since you completed that worksheet.

Then review the **Identify Your Triggers** worksheet from this chapter, and consider whether any of these triggers are interfering with your goals. Which goals are being blocked by the way your amygdala responds to these triggers? This can help you identify which triggers you would like to focus on first. You may even think of more triggers to add to your list as you consider your goals. For example, it wasn't until Anton thought about his goal of interviewing for a new job that he realized that the trigger of making direct eye contact with a stranger was interfering with this goal.

The following chart will help you in this process. Write down at least three goals you'd like to accomplish and the triggers blocking those goals. Then use the **Rating Your Anxiety** worksheet from chapter 1 to assess how much anxiety you typically experience in relation to each trigger.

Goal	Trigger(s) Blocking Goal	Anxiety Score(s)

Answers to the Diagramming Triggers Worksheet

1. Trigger: Bald/shaved head   Negative event = Sexual assault

2. Trigger: Tree/trees   Negative event = Lightning/explosion

3. Trigger: Sitting in front   Negative event = Being teased

Chapter 10

Teaching the Amygdala through Exposure

When you feel the defense response, whether it's in the form of nausea, a nagging sense of anxiety, a desire to escape, or a full-blown panic attack, wouldn't it be wonderful to be able to turn that response off? Wouldn't you like to be able to explain to your amygdala that the defense response is not necessary and that dealing with physical discomfort and anxiety is interfering with your life? Although the amygdala cannot be controlled or influenced by logical explanations, you have learned that there *is* a way to teach it to respond differently: by pairing your trigger with a new learning experience. Whether your trigger is a spider, an attentive audience awaiting your performance, or the sound of explosions, you can teach your amygdala to stop producing the defense response to that trigger.

For example, after Rodney had a very bad experience presenting his science project in middle school, speaking in front of a group of people became a trigger for him. Anytime he had to speak in front of a group, he felt very anxious and uncomfortable. In his history class, he even took an F on an assignment rather than give a speech on the Civil War. But there was one teacher who helped his amygdala learn a new association: Mrs. Criner. She taught a rhetoric class where she encouraged every student to do a weekly presentation, and she made the experience so enjoyable and amusing that Rodney got over his fear of public speaking. After repeatedly speaking in front of the class—with nothing negative occurring and, in fact, his fellow students applauding him—Rodney's amygdala began to respond differently.

As we noted, this process of deliberately presenting a trigger to ourselves is called *exposure*. Exposure uses the language of association to teach the amygdala to respond differently. The amygdala may have learned to identify an object as dangerous when it was previously paired with a negative event, but if that pairing no longer occurs, the amygdala can learn to respond differently. In exposure, you deliberately spend time around the trigger, making sure it is *not* paired with a negative experience, in order to activate the neural circuitry you want to change. Just as you need hot water to make tea, you need activated circuitry to make change in the amygdala.

Often, people mistakenly believe they've tried exposure when they've exposed themselves to their trigger on just one occasion. However, in exposure, the trigger is presented not just once, but *multiple* times until the person can remain in the situation with little or no anxiety. One neutral or positive experience in the presence of a trigger is not enough to teach the amygdala; repeated presentations are necessary. In addition, if you want to teach someone's amygdala that a trigger is not dangerous, it is very important that the person isn't harmed, ridiculed, or put in any sort of danger (or threat of danger) during the process. Those kinds of experiences will only serve to reinforce what the amygdala previously learned.

However, one negative thing *will* happen during the exposure process, which you may have already realized. The person is going to experience feelings of anxiety, fear, and distress during the exposure. That's because a trigger is, by definition, something that causes the amygdala to produce the defense response; there is no way to expose the amygdala to a trigger without experiencing some distress or discomfort at first. Exposure is a no pain, no gain situation. You will need to stay in the exposure until your fear and anxiety go down, as uncomfortable as that might be. If you continue avoiding your triggers, you'll make it impossible for your amygdala to learn and change. Although avoiding triggers comes very naturally—as humans, we try not to encounter or stay in the presence of anything that causes distress or discomfort—avoidance allows the amygdala to continue controlling your life. Your ability to achieve your goals can become more and more restricted. Therefore, when you see avoidance interfering with your goals, recognize that exposure is the answer.

Although this can be challenging, hopefully you understand that your amygdala cannot learn anything new if it doesn't stay in the presence of a trigger long enough to recognize that nothing negative is occurring. It's important to stay in the exposure and to trust that your fear and anxiety *will* eventually go down, as it is physically impossible for your body to remain in an activated state forever. The amygdala is designed to learn, and it will stop producing the defense response when it recognizes that no danger exists. Open yourself up to the experience of discomfort and resist the urge to escape. Tell yourself, "I am staying in the exposure until my amygdala learns it is safe to be around this trigger."

As your amygdala learns, you will actually experience it! You will feel the anxiety and other aspects of the defense response decreasing, which can be very empowering. I have had clients say, "I didn't know I could do this! I just have to stay in the situation, and the amygdala learns!" Even if you have feared a specific trigger for years or decades, a new and positive experience with this trigger will provide your amygdala with the updated information it needs in order to learn. It can be comforting to know that the distress of going through the experience will pay off. Another way to recognize the amygdala's learning process is to use the **Rating Your Anxiety** worksheet from chapter 1 to assess how you react to your triggers as you go through the process of exposure, observing how your scores change from when you rated these triggers at the end of chapter 9.

You may find that simply *thinking* about your triggers is beginning to cause you to experience some distress. This is normal and actually shows that you are already getting the amygdala's attention. Oftentimes, the first step of exposure can be to think about your trigger before considering facing it head on. If you push through the anxiety, you will find that your amygdala will eventually become more comfortable with these thoughts. You will be able to imagine your triggers with less anxiety, changing your amygdala in the process!

Although many people expect that making a change to the amygdala will take a very long time, you can often feel a change occur in a matter of minutes. For example, one client sat behind the steering wheel of a parked car in order to get over her fear of driving, and she was surprised that it took less than 10 minutes for her to feel a decrease in her anxiety: "I expected to be sitting here an hour before I could feel a change!" While the time it takes for the amygdala to learn depends on the person and the situation, it rarely takes more than 45 minutes (and frequently less than 15 minutes) to feel a change in your anxiety, if exposure is used correctly.

However, exposing yourself to your trigger a single time is not enough for the amygdala to experience new learning. The amygdala needs enough exposure to form new emotional memories, not just turn off the defense response. Therefore, multiple, repeated exposures are necessary, with the number of necessary exposures varying as a function of how traumatic the original learning experience was. For example, the amygdala will learn more quickly if the trigger involves being stung by an insect, as opposed to experiencing a sexual assault.

That's why I strongly recommend that you start with the help of a therapist trained in exposure therapy: to make sure you use exposure correctly. Exposure sessions need to be long enough in duration and close enough in time so that learning occurs. If you do exposure incorrectly, it can actually result in an increase in anxiety, rather than a decrease. Not all therapists have been trained in exposure therapy, so you will need to specifically ask about this technique. Even though it is possible to do exposure on your own, it is more difficult to attend to the important details of this process without guidance. (Remember, you will likely be feeling distress during the early stages of exposure). When an experienced therapist is involved, exposure therapy has been shown to be especially effective and works more rapidly (Lang & Helbig-Lang, 2012).

Selecting a Trigger to Begin With

Look back at the **Identifying Triggers That Block Your Goals** worksheet at the end of chapter 9. Choose one goal that is important to you—this is the goal you will start working on first. If you're having trouble selecting a goal, consider a situation you deal with frequently or one which creates the most difficulty in your life. In any case, focus your efforts on a goal that will make a real difference to you. Exposure is not easy, and you need to get a reward from going through the challenging process!

After you choose a goal, select one trigger that is associated with that goal. Choose a trigger that is moderately anxiety provoking, but not extremely anxiety provoking, for your first exposure experience. You will be most successful if you get some practice with exposure and experience the challenges and benefits of the process *before* taking on your most challenging triggers. Once you have selected a trigger, you are ready to begin teaching your amygdala something new. Remind yourself that the amygdala has stored certain information about this trigger in the circuitry in your brain, and you need to design a learning experience for the amygdala that will teach it to make new circuitry.

Teaching the Amygdala That a Trigger Is Safe

As you start the process of exposure, your cortex and your amygdala are probably not on the same page. That's because your cortex—the logical, thinking part of your brain—realizes that your reactions to the trigger don't always make sense. In turn, you may feel embarrassed that you can't control your responses or think yourself out of your difficulties. You may even find it difficult to explain to others why this trigger is such a barrier in your life. However, it's important to remember that your cortex and amygdala see the trigger differently. Even though your cortex can understand the situation more logically, your amygdala creates strong emotional and physical reactions.

You should not trust the amygdala, however. Remember that the amygdala reacts to incomplete knowledge in comparison to the cortex, which processes sensory information in a great deal more detail by adding in knowledge, logic, and memories. What is confusing is that you feel the same reaction regardless of whether the situation is a truly dangerous one or whether the amygdala has misinterpreted or overestimated the danger in the situation. In fact, the cortex may start focusing on these reactions and generate thoughts that add to your distress, causing the defense response to take over even more. It is easy to begin to believe that you are in danger on the basis of what is happening in your body.

In order to take back control of your life, you need to teach your amygdala to respond differently to the trigger. Fill in the blanks here with your trigger and your goal:

I am going to teach my amygdala to stop reacting to:

_____

_____

in ways that keep me from:

_____

_____.

Getting through the exposure will be a challenging experience, so the next thing you'll want to do is create an *exposure hierarchy*, which is an ordered list of steps that will allow you to approach the trigger in a gradual manner. By breaking down the process into a series of steps, you can approach it at a pace and a level of intensity that feels comfortable to you so you can better navigate the uncomfortable emotions that are a normal part of the exposure process. Exposure will work whether you approach it in a gradual way or a more intense way. You don't have to experience a high level of distress for the amygdala to learn and form new neural circuits, though higher anxiety during exposure can speed the process of change (Cahill et al., 2006). The following worksheet will help you create your exposure hierarchy.

Creating an Exposure Hierarchy

First, consider the specific trigger you have decided to work on, and think of the *most* anxiety-provoking situation you want to be able to tolerate with regard to that trigger. This won't necessarily be the most terrifying experience you can possibly imagine; it should be something you actually want to accomplish. For example, Simone, a landscape architect, is afraid that a snake will fall off a branch and onto her shoulder as she tags a tree, which is a routine task in her job. Therefore, she might write, "having a snake on my shoulder." This is a realistic goal that would greatly reduce her anxiety in the field (unlike, say, "being trapped on an airplane with hundreds of snakes," which is terrifying, but not realistic or necessary for Simone!). Using the template provided, write down your most anxiety-provoking (but realistic) situation as the *last* step of the hierarchy.

Next, focus on a behavior or situation that would elicit *some* anxiety but that you feel you could readily accomplish if you were to push yourself. Simone might say, "Seeing a snake in a cage is stressful, but I could handle that." Write down this least anxiety-provoking situation as the *first* step in your exposure hierarchy.

Now you're ready to list other anxiety-provoking activities that could come in between these two anchoring points. Write down between 5 and 10 different situations, objects, or behaviors that would cause you to experience distress in relation to the trigger. Don't worry about putting these steps in order yet—just brainstorm. Some of the steps could look pretty similar, except for an important detail that would increase the level of anxiety you would feel. Simone may experience differing levels of anxiety if she stands 10 feet away from a caged snake versus just one foot away. Describe each step clearly to show how it is different from the others.

After you've completed your list, rate the distress you would feel in each situation using a scale of 0 to 100, where 0 is no distress and 100 is the worst distress you can image experiencing. This is known as your subjective units of distress (SUDs) level, and it takes into account any anxiety, physical discomfort, or distressing thoughts you would experience in response to these situations. SUDs ratings reflect how you personally react to each situation, so your ratings are unique to you. In a way, you are trying to judge just how much *your* amygdala will react to each specific situation. My clients sometimes say, "My amygdala is not going to like this one at all!"

After you have rated each activity, write them down on your exposure hierarchy in order from lowest to highest SUDs. The order of these activities will not necessarily be logical; it is based on your reaction to each situation. After completing your hierarchy, look at your SUDs ratings in the right-hand column. If you find a large increase from one step to the next, see if you can think of a situation or behavior that would get a SUDs rating in between those steps, and insert that step between the other two. This helps you avoid having a large "jump" in difficulty as you work through the hierarchy. The number of steps in an exposure hierarchy can vary, but you should aim for 10 or fewer.

Here is Simone's exposure hierarchy as an example, followed by a blank template for your own use.

Step	Activity	SUDs (0–100)
1	Seeing a snake in a cage from 10 feet away	20
2	Seeing a snake in a cage from 1 foot away	35
3	Seeing a snake outside its cage while someone else holds it	45
4	Seeing a snake outside its cage on the ground, moving around	60
5	Holding a snake in my hands while someone else holds it too	75
6	Having a snake in my lap without touching it	85
7	Having a snake on my shoulder without touching it	95

Step	Activity	SUDs (0–100)
1		
2		
3		
4		
5		
6		
7		

Space to Brainstorm Activities

_____

_____

_____

_____

_____

_____

No doubt there are a variety of reasons why you have not attempted or completed exposure to your trigger before. Therefore, once you have developed your hierarchy, take some time to consider your thoughts related to facing these exposure steps. If you find that you have any worrisome thoughts, I recommend talking with your therapist about them. Be honest about any negative thoughts you are having, and work through any that may interfere with your willingness to carry out exposures. In the next two chapters, I'll also discuss ways to combat thoughts that may activate the amygdala and work against you when you are trying to teach the amygdala that the situation is safe.

Exposure Guidelines

In order to make exposure sessions effective, here are some helpful guidelines to remember during the process. Use them to help you tame that amygdala!

Carefully plan and monitor your progress throughout the exposure process. You and your therapist can use your exposure hierarchy to design exposures that will retrain your amygdala to stop activating in response to the trigger. The goal is to gradually expose yourself to the steps in this hierarchy, working from lower levels to higher levels, until the trigger no longer causes you distress. Although you can start with the lowest activity on your hierarchy, I recommend starting with an activity that has a SUDs level around 40, if possible, for a couple of reasons: (1) Most people can handle getting through situations rated below 40 without much trouble or special training, and (2) activities at this level have a high enough SUDs rating to allow you to clearly feel a decrease in distress when your amygdala begins to learn. It is very empowering to feel, as you get through the steps, that you are teaching the amygdala to respond differently and making a lasting change in your brain.

The SUDs rating is also a very helpful measure *during* the exposure process. You can use it to identify and communicate what level of distress you are feeling during the exposure at any given time, as well as how it changes over time. Rate your distress every couple of minutes so you and your therapist are aware of how the exposure is progressing. Although your distress level may go up beyond what you expected when you first rated the situation, *it is essential that you do not leave the situation until your anxiety has decreased.* Otherwise, you are teaching your amygdala that escape is needed, which will cause it to produce an even greater defense response the next time you encounter the trigger.

The goal is to stay in the situation until your SUDs rating comes down to *at least half* of the highest rating you experienced in the session. That means if your highest rating is a 50, getting to a 25 is sufficient. This level of change helps you recognize that the amygdala has learned and has stopped producing the defense response. You may choose to stay in the exposure longer, but it is never necessary for your SUDs rating to go to 0. Remember that, even after the amygdala stops producing the defense response, some aspects of the response, such as the effects of adrenaline or some muscle stiffness, may linger.

Continue to work through each step of the hierarchy over multiple exposure trials until you can complete that step with confidence and little to no distress. Make sure you plan in advance to give yourself *multiple* opportunities to practice each step in the hierarchy. Exposures must be done repeatedly for your amygdala to learn most effectively. Repeated exposures help your brain build new neural circuits that no longer associate the trigger with distress. Each time you repeat the exposure, you will likely find that the particular step becomes easier, and your amygdala turns off the defense response more quickly.

Make sure you are properly and directly experiencing the trigger. It's important that you don't distract yourself from the feared situation or object during the exposure. You need to allow yourself to fully experience the trigger—directly looking at, listening to, and sometimes even feeling or smelling it—so the amygdala can respond to it and, ultimately, learn not to associate it with any danger. When you feel your heart pound or your muscles tense up, know that you have definitely gotten the amygdala's attention and that the exposure is going well. One of my clients, who was working to overcome his fear of heights, told me during his exposure session that he wanted to look over the ledge of the top floor of the parking garage. He was really showing his amygdala the whole experience.

Remember your relaxation skills. The relaxation skills you learned in chapter 6— like deep breathing and muscle relaxation—will help you handle the stress of the exposure and will send your amygdala a message of calmness. Remember, however, that it's unlikely you will be able to relax yourself completely, given that your amygdala naturally produces the defense response in reaction to this trigger. In addition, you *want* to keep your amygdala somewhat activated because new wiring cannot develop unless the amygdala is firing. You need to activate the amygdala to generate new connections, which means that, until your amygdala learns to respond differently, you will experience distress each time you encounter the trigger. Your therapist can coach you through the process of using relaxation skills to keep your distress at a manageable level so you can stay in the situation.

Consider using imaginal exposure. If you're having difficulty trying an actual step in your hierarchy, you can begin by *imagining* yourself in the situation instead. For example, Justin was so worried about doing exposures with an actual dog that he first needed to imagine himself being in the presence of a dog until he reduced his distress enough to try real-life exposures. This process, which is known as *imaginal exposure*, also activates the amygdala because the amygdala often responds to thoughts or images of a trigger in the same way it would to a real trigger. If you're working with a therapist, they may guide you through this process by describing the imagined situation in great detail. You can also do imaginal exposure by simply picturing yourself in the anxiety-provoking situation, taking care to imagine specific sights, sounds, and smells you might encounter. When you can successfully imagine situations without much distress, you are making changes to the amygdala.

In some cases, imaginal exposure is the only way to do exposure. For example, I have used imaginal exposure when working with Gulf War veterans who were trying to cope with nightmares of combat experiences and with clients who had fears I couldn't recreate in session, like becoming pregnant, losing a child to cancer, or asking the boss for a raise. There are also some situations where real-life exposure would not be ethical (e.g., asking a pharmacist with a fear of dispensing the wrong medicine to do so). Sometimes I'll record an exposure script that the client can listen to repeatedly. Although imaginal exposure can be an effective treatment that builds confidence and reduces distress, when possible, the best treatment is still for the amygdala to *directly* experience the trigger in a safe environment.

Carefully monitor and manage your thoughts during the exposure session. Do not unnecessarily increase your distress by engaging in thoughts that are self-defeating ("I'll never be able to do this!") or amygdala activating ("I'm going to lose control of the car and get in an accident") because they increase your SUDs level rather than helping decrease it. When you engage in these thoughts, you are not teaching the amygdala that the situation is safe; you are doing just the opposite. Stay focused on what is happening and what you are experiencing *in the moment*, rather than anticipating what could possibly occur. We'll discuss how to address amygdala-activating thoughts in the next two chapters, but here are some general coping thoughts that will be useful during exposure:

- "Keep breathing deeply. This won't last long."

- "I expect my distress to rise, but I can manage it."

- "I want this distress to occur because it means the amygdala is paying attention."

- "Release the tension; just relax my muscles as much as possible."

- "This won't last too long. If I wait, the amygdala will learn."

- "I'm taking control by teaching my amygdala there is nothing to fear."

- "My amygdala doesn't like this, but I can handle it."

- "When I get through this, my amygdala won't always react this way."

- "Stay focused on this situation. This is all I have to deal with right now."

Mindfulness can help you fully experience and benefit from exposure. To be mindful as the amygdala produces the defense response is to notice what parts of your body are reacting and to identify them to yourself: "My heart is pounding harder. I'm getting slightly nauseous." Be curious, observant, and accepting of what you are experiencing, rather than trying to fight or judge the process. Don't expect to stay in control of your bodily responses; it is not your goal to keep the body from reacting. Let the amygdala do whatever it does and just wait.

Simply watch what your body is doing from the wiser perspective of understanding what is happening in your amygdala: "What are you doing now, amygdala? You are tensing up my muscles, like you want me to run or fight." These reactions make sense in a dangerous situation, but remember this situation is safe. Notice also when you feel a change in what the amygdala is doing: "I'm finding it easier to breathe deeply. I think the amygdala is recognizing this isn't such a big deal." By staying in the exposure, you are teaching your amygdala that its reactions to the trigger are not necessary.

Be aware of the danger of safety-seeking behaviors. Safety-seeking behaviors are actions you engage in to help you get through a difficult situation but that prevent the amygdala from learning. For example, if you bring a bottle of tranquilizing medication with you to the mall so you can take a pill in case you feel overwhelmed, having that bottle of medicine (even if you don't take any) may prevent your amygdala from learning that the situation is safe. The amygdala is learning to go to the mall with the bottle of medication, not to reduce the fear of going to the mall.

Other examples include having a friend or family member with you (or on the phone with you) during the anxiety-provoking experience, carrying a lucky charm or object that helps you feel safe, always sitting near the door, or wearing sunglasses or avoiding eye contact with others. Safety-seeking behaviors provide a temporary crutch instead of changing the amygdala's response to the trigger, so it's important that you do not resort to these behaviors during exposure.

Response prevention may be necessary. If you have learned certain responses, rituals, or checking behaviors to cope with your fears, worries, or distress, you need to eliminate these from exposure sessions. For example, Lorraine was able to drive on busy streets as long as she held her hands in a certain position on the steering wheel; driving with one hand, even for a moment, felt unsafe. If you have learned to perform a particular response in order to feel safe, and you use that in exposure, it only strengthens the amygdala's assumption that the trigger is dangerous. Not performing the response is the only way you can retrain the amygdala. When we prohibit the use of a specific ritual or response while a person is being exposed to a trigger, we call it *exposure with response prevention*. This kind of exposure is often used to effectively treat OCD, such as when a person is asked not to use hand sanitizer every time they touch money.

Avoid medications that can interfere with exposure. Medications such as benzodiazepines have been shown to interfere with exposure (Rothbaum et al., 2014; van Minnen et al., 2002; Sudak, 2011) because they inhibit (or sedate) neurons in various parts of the body, including the amygdala, which prevents it from being activated. While this can block the amygdala from creating the defense response (which is often why people take benzodiazepines), it also prevents the amygdala from making any new connections. In other words, no learning occurs in the amygdala. The person is likely to get through the exposure session with less distress, but the exposure will not be effective in changing the amygdala's response to the trigger.

Avoid seeking reassurance. The goal of exposure is to show the amygdala that you are safe in the situation, so it is counterproductive to repeatedly seek reassurance when you are in the presence of the trigger. It undermines all the hard work you are doing. If someone is constantly reassuring you during the exposure, what will you do when you encounter the trigger on your own? What you need is not for someone to tell you that you're safe but, rather, for them to tell you that you can handle what you are going through. For example, if during the exposure you ask, "The dog won't get too close?" your therapist might say, "We agreed the dog wouldn't touch you this time, but it could come close. You just handle whatever comes." You need to *show* the amygdala that the trigger is safe, not tell it. I should also note that the need for reassurance is often connected to a need to have certainty, and we all need to learn to cope with the uncertainty of life instead of pretending we can know how everything will turn out.

You are allowed to complain. As you are going through the exposure process, you can verbalize how much you hate it or how hard it is. You do not have to pretend that it is easy or that you have no discomfort. You are deliberately allowing yourself to experience distressful—and sometimes overwhelming—emotions and sensations, and even though they are not dangerous, you are enduring a dreadful situation. I find that I need to acknowledge to my clients that exposure is definitely difficult and unpleasant and that they are doing a great job sticking with it. I remind them that courage is not the absence of fear; it is acting in the face of fear. Remember that no emotion lasts forever. It will eventually pass if you endure it.

Resist any temptation to leave the presence of the trigger until your distress goes down. If you end the exposure while you are still feeling a strong defense response, it reinforces the idea that escape is the right response and keeps the amygdala from learning that the situation is safe. You need to experience a reduction in distress *while still in the presence of the trigger* in order for learning to occur. Wait for your discomfort to decrease, remembering that this is an opportunity to put yourself—instead of the amygdala—in the driver's seat. Your amygdala can and will change if you are willing to push through the distress.

If you do need to leave the exposure, commit yourself to coming back and getting through the situation. It is normal to have a setback or two. You still have the opportunity to teach the amygdala; it is always able to learn. Remember, the goal is not just about overcoming the influence of your amygdala in this specific moment. You are staying in the situation to make long-lasting changes in your neural circuitry that will allow you to achieve your goals.

Work toward being independent in exposure situations. The goal of exposure is to help you and your amygdala become comfortable with the trigger. This means that, ultimately, you will need to handle exposure situations on your own, without the help of a therapist, family member, or friend. (An exception would be if the trigger itself involves being in a situation with someone else, like when my client's goal was to fly on a plane to the Virgin Islands with his new wife on their honeymoon.)

Therefore, you should plan to get through certain exposure steps by yourself, which means you will need to do homework assignments between therapy sessions. My clients have accomplished a variety of exposures without my being there, including driving independently, going to movies with friends, interviewing for jobs, and attending drag shows in a bar. Make plans to carry out exposures by yourself out in the real world so you can follow your own goals and teach your amygdala to stop interfering with the life you want.

When you complete each step in the exposure hierarchy, take some time to consider what you learned. After you get through an exposure experience, ask yourself if your worries came true and, if so, how you handled them. Look for changes in how you responded, and consider what you learned about your amygdala and yourself. What did you do that worked? What would change next time? What surprised you about the experience? Your therapist can also provide feedback on what you did well and what strategies you can use to improve next time.

Reward yourself. Doing exposure is hard work, so you should celebrate your achievements along the way. When you complete a step in your exposure hierarchy, congratulate yourself and treat yourself to something special. You deserve it!

Build on your success. Once you successfully complete the last step on your exposure hierarchy—the one with highest SUDs rating—you are typically ready to work on the life goal you set for yourself. Since you have made changes to the way your amygdala reacts, you should find that your trigger no longer blocks you from achieving this goal. After seeing how exposure helps you achieve this specific goal, you can choose another goal to work toward, using exposure to keep your amygdala from blocking you from living the life you want to live.

Chapter 11

How Your Cortex Can
Activate Your Amygdala

You have learned how much influence your amygdala can have over your life, but you've also learned how to calm your amygdala and even ways to teach it to respond differently to triggers. But sometimes, the amygdala is not where the anxiety *begins*. At times, certain thoughts in your cortex may cause the amygdala to become activated, which then produces an anxiety response. Therefore, if you want to keep your amygdala healthy and calm, you also need to know about the relationship between the amygdala and the cortex.

By now you know that the amygdala is the part of our brain that creates feelings of fear, panic, and anxiety—the cortex cannot create these feelings on its own. That's why the cortex pathway to anxiety also includes the amygdala as part of that pathway (refer back to figure 3 in chapter 4 for a reminder of the cortex pathway). When you consider the different regions that make up our brain, it's important to remember that they are not independent structures that work in isolation of each other. Rather, our brain regions are connected to one another via a complex web of neural circuits, including those that exist between the amygdala and the cortex.

Therefore, what happens in the cortex does not stay in the cortex. Just as the amygdala is always scanning our environment for any indication of danger, it is also constantly scanning the cortex. When the cortex receives information from the thalamus, the cortex processes this information to produce a variety of thoughts and images, which are then carefully monitored by the amygdala. In fact, the amygdala has many more connections going into the cortex than the cortex has going down to the amygdala (LeDoux, 1996). I explain the relationship between these two brain regions by saying, "The amygdala is watching cortex television." When the amygdala is observing thoughts or images of a distressing situation produced in the cortex, these thoughts and images can prompt the amygdala to activate the defense response, causing us to feel anxiety, fear, or even panic.

Although the amygdala pathway to anxiety is always operating—even at the same time as the cortex pathway—the amygdala sometimes doesn't react to the information it receives as if it is significant until the cortex has processed it. In other words, the amygdala can receive the same sensory information as the cortex but not recognize the potential threat that information represents until the cortex has provided more context. That's why the cortex pathway to anxiety is so important.

Here's an example to illustrate this process. In Melinda's apartment, the smoke alarm was hardwired into the electrical system. The smoke alarm was faulty, and dust buildup or even a spider walking across one of the smoke detectors would set off the alarm. The landlord had promised to replace it, but it wasn't a simple repair, and Melinda had to endure several weeks of the alarm going off at odd and inconvenient times. Her amygdala became accustomed to the sound and did not consider it a danger signal, even though it was annoying. In order to turn off the alarm, Melinda had to go downstairs and flip the breaker to reset the system. One night, Melinda had fallen asleep on the couch when the smoke alarm went off. She got up in a daze and went to flip the breaker so the sound would stop. But then she remembered that she had lit a candle in her bedroom, and she wondered if something upstairs could have caught fire.

Melinda suddenly felt her fear kick in, and she became wide awake. The thoughts in her cortex had gotten her amygdala's attention! She ran upstairs to her room and found that some artificial flowers near the candle had caught fire, but she grabbed them and threw them in the bathtub before the fire spread. Luckily, Melinda's cortex had detected this danger. Her amygdala had not responded to the smoke alarm until her cortex developed these thoughts. The amygdala only responded to the potential *meaning* of the alarm, which her cortex developed, not to the sound of the alarm itself. Therefore, in this case, Melinda's amygdala was activated through the cortex pathway. I think you will agree it is helpful that the amygdala monitors the cortex this way so it can detect any threats that it would otherwise not recognize.

The sensory information that the amygdala gets from the thalamus is raw and unprocessed, so it doesn't always have complete and accurate information. Remember that the cortex pathway takes longer than the amygdala pathway, so it is possible for the amygdala to react before the cortex has completed processing the information. In chapter 4, we saw how this happened with Daniel in the fraternity house: His amygdala reacted to the toy rat in the freezer before his cortex had a chance to provide the detailed information that it was a toy. In Melinda's case, the amygdala only reacted after the cortex interpreted the incoming sensory information with more details—including information from her memory—and produced amygdala-activating thoughts.

In addition to using memory and logic to consider whether danger was present, if Melinda has a good imagination, her cortex could even have supplemented the sensory input by creating images that went beyond the information it received, like imagining her bedroom in flames. The amygdala's ability to monitor thoughts and images in the cortex can be very useful in allowing the amygdala to detect threats it may not recognize without the cortex's help.

Cortex Influences on Amygdala Activation

In general, the cortex can activate the amygdala in two ways. The first is **by providing detailed information about sensory experiences** and combining this with any other information that the cortex associates with these sensory experiences. Consider Nate, who has been having difficulties with his girlfriend. They have been arguing over issues that have come up in their long-distance relationship, and he knows she is unhappy. Whenever his phone buzzes and he sees he has a text from his girlfriend, Nate immediately worries that she is going to break up with him. He feels nauseous and his heart starts pounding. Although Nate is experiencing the effects of amygdala activation, his amygdala is not reacting to the buzz of the phone or the notification that a text message has arrived. The thoughts in Nate's cortex—which interpret the text message to mean that a breakup is coming—activate the amygdala (figure 10).

However, it's important to note that the cortex's interpretations are not always correct. When Nate opened a recent text message from his girlfriend, he realized that she had simply sent him a picture of a term paper on which she got an A. His amygdala had become activated in response to the cortex's faulty interpretation. We'll discuss how the cortex can frequently misconstrue incoming information later in this chapter.

Figure 10

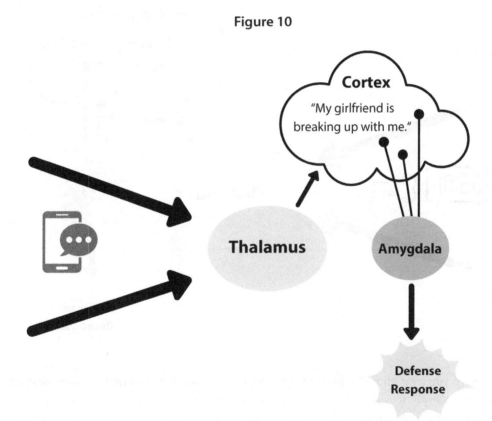

The second way the cortex can activate the amygdala is **by creating thoughts or images in the absence of any sensory information**. Even when there is no incoming sensory information to suggest that a threat exists, the cortex can still imagine a threat. While we take the ability to have thoughts like these for granted, humans are uniquely able to conjure up thoughts and worries.

As an example, consider Alma, who recently adopted a German shepherd puppy, Ranger. Knowing how large Ranger would get, she didn't want to teach him to sleep in bed with her. Each night, she put Ranger in his little dog bed next to hers, but he often whimpered and whined, wanting to be lifted into the bed. One night, Alma finally managed to fall asleep in spite of his whining, only to wake up suddenly and realize it was 5:00 a.m. A peaceful silence reigned, but instead of being happy, Alma's cortex imagined that something had happened to Ranger, which caused her amygdala to produce the defense response (figure 11). She quickly checked Ranger's bed and found him curled up and sleeping peacefully. Although Alma's thought was not based on any sensory information, it still activated the amygdala, producing feelings of distress. In fact, as Alma looked down at her sleeping puppy, she still had a pounding heart and a sick feeling in her stomach.

Figure 11

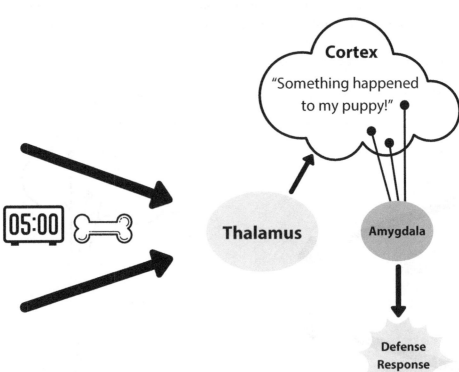

Have you ever thought back to a frightening event that occurred in your past and found that simply recalling this event caused you to feel a rush of anxiety? Or have you imagined a stressful situation that might occur in the future and found that your heart started pounding? The amygdala's ability to respond to mere thoughts as though a danger were present gives you a different understanding of your anxiety. In some cases, thoughts about the past or future can be helpful, even though the amygdala produces a defense response in reaction to these thoughts. For example, if you're worrying about an upcoming presentation at work and begin to feel anxious, it focuses your attention on the presentation and could potentially motivate you to spend time preparing and considering how to respond to criticisms or questions that you anticipate.

However, we sometimes anticipate situations that are very unlikely (for example, fearing that you'll make a mistake during the presentation that will result in your being fired), and we experience unnecessary or excessive distress for no reason. This is because the amygdala doesn't have a way to determine the difference between unsubstantiated thoughts about a potential danger and thoughts that actually indicate a true threat exists. For example, when Ricardo is preparing to leave for work and thinks about getting into a car accident on the snowy roads, his amygdala reacts as if this has actually happened or will happen, even though he is still in his warm kitchen, drinking his coffee. As a result, Ricardo now feels anxious about driving. The amygdala often treats thoughts as if they are a direct indication of danger, rather than simply thoughts, and we feel a very real experience of anxiety as a result.

Does Your Anxiety Often Start in the Cortex?

To determine whether your cortex is producing thoughts that activate your amygdala, consider the following questions, and put a check mark next to those that apply to you:

- ❏ Do you tend to think about ways that a situation could turn out badly?
- ❏ Do you tend to anticipate ways that people might judge or criticize you?
- ❏ Do you hold yourself to very high standards that are difficult to reach?
- ❏ Do you have the tendency to imagine very distressing occurrences?
- ❏ Do people consider you to be a pessimist or a worrier?
- ❏ Do you have difficulty letting go of past difficulties or mistakes?
- ❏ Do you frequently worry about potential illnesses or injuries?
- ❏ Do you experience distress when you have doubts or can't feel certain about something?
- ❏ Do you have thoughts that you consider to be unacceptable?
- ❏ Do you tend to think the worst when you have a physical symptom?

If you checked off more than three of these questions, your amygdala is likely experiencing frequent activation as a result of the thoughts created in your cortex. Remember that the amygdala is constantly watching "cortex television," and when the channel is playing a marathon of negative thoughts or images, the amygdala will react to them. While this can be helpful in some situations, like when Melinda's flowers caught fire, you may often be experiencing unnecessary anxiety if your cortex has a tendency to produce distressing thoughts or images that don't reflect reality. In this chapter, you'll learn how to keep your cortex from activating your amygdala when it is not necessary.

Cognitive Therapy and the Cortex

Before neuroscientists even knew the amygdala's role in anxiety, some therapists had recognized the importance of cognitions in producing emotional reactions. *Cognition* is the psychological term for the mental processes that most people refer to as "thinking."

Cognitive therapists proposed that anxiety can be created or worsened by certain types of thinking (Beck, 1976; Ellis, 2016). These therapists focused on the beliefs that people have about themselves, others, and the world, including how these beliefs influence the way people interpret events. They recognized that we all sometimes distort reality in our thinking processes by overestimating danger or having unrealistic expectations.

For example, Candice can be perfectly safe, drinking her breakfast tea at her kitchen table, while also experiencing a high level of dread as she imagines what could happen to her dog, Sadie, if she can't afford the surgery Sadie needs. Similarly, Marcia might experience anxiety whenever she writes an email because she worries that others will judge her grammar and punctuation and will react critically to any mistake she makes. Cognitive therapists help people to change these kinds of thoughts by changing the processes that occur in the cortex, which allows the person to have more control over their emotional reactions.

You might be wondering whether changing your thoughts can really prevent anxiety. Sometimes it can—when these thoughts caused your amygdala to produce the anxiety response in the first place. In other words, working to modify unhelpful thoughts can be effective when anxiety is coming from the cortex pathway. This is especially the case for particular anxiety-based disorders, such as OCD, generalized anxiety disorder, and social anxiety disorder, which are heavily influenced by cortex-initiated anxiety. But remember that the amygdala can also produce anxiety through the amygdala pathway, without any involvement of the cortex at all. When anxiety seems to come directly from exposure to an object or situation, and you don't feel like you have been worrying or thinking about anything, or when anxiety seems to appear out of the blue or seems very strong for the situation at hand, the amygdala pathway is usually the source. But if your anxiety often starts in the cortex, cognitive therapy approaches can be very helpful.

Interpretations in the Cortex

When the cortex processes what you see, it doesn't just give you an image or a name of whatever you are seeing. Your cortex senses, perceives, and interprets this sensory information, and it's this *interpretation* that strongly influences how your amygdala reacts, not the situation or event itself. Consider when Candice let her dog, Sadie, out into the yard one morning, not realizing that the wind from an overnight storm had knocked down a portion of the fence. When Candice tried to call Sadie back in, she realized Sadie was not in the yard. Candice immediately worried that Sadie was wandering loose in the neighborhood and would either get hit by a car or become lost forever. Candice searched for Sadie for almost an hour while experiencing dreadful anxiety. Luckily, she found Sadie sitting on the Richardsons' back porch, hoping for some ear scratches and a piece of cheese from her favorite neighbors. It was Candice's interpretation of what *could* have happened to Sadie—not the sight of the empty yard—that led her to experience anxiety (figure 12). In this case, Candice's amygdala activation started with her thoughts about what could have happened to Sadie.

Figure 12

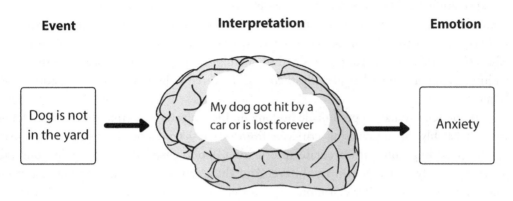

Has this type of situation ever happened to you, where you made an interpretation of a situation that later turned out to be wrong? Too many times we accept our thoughts as indicators of reality and forget that the cortex can be prone to misinterpretations or false conclusions. Like the amygdala's faulty signals, the cortex's interpretations can be equally untrustworthy. In fact, we can't even trust what the cortex *sees*. The cortex literally sees things that are not there and also misses things that are clearly present. Figure 13 illustrates this phenomenon. If you see a white triangle in the picture, you are being fooled by the cortex, which is filling in some information that is not really there. There is no white triangle, despite what your cortex tells you. In addition, if you read the information in the star, you may find that your cortex has kept you from seeing something that is clearly there. (You may need to look more than once to see it.) If you can't even trust the visual information your cortex creates, can you always trust your thoughts?

Figure 13

As this shows, your cortex *constructs* reality; it does not simply reflect reality. Based on its expectations, it fills in details that may not be accurate or leaves out information that is important. Your cortex can even take a nonsense sentence and make it seem readable to you. Try to read this: Wehn popele turst teihr crotxe, tehy aer otfen srupirsed to raelzie taht teh'rye otfen foloed. Your cortex actively manipulates what you are seeing, rather than faithfully showing you what is really there—so be careful about what interpretations you believe.

If you tend to have a pessimistic outlook on life—always expecting the worst, judging yourself harshly, or anticipating criticism from others—remember that your cortex may not be providing you with accurate information about what is happening in your life or what is likely to happen in the future. And these faulty interpretations are activating your amygdala and causing you more distress than is necessary. The good news is that by learning to question and change your cortex's interpretation of the situation, you can often reduce your anxiety. I will explain this strategy more in the next chapter.

The Anxiety Channel

As I've mentioned, your cortex is like cable television, except that your cortex has *millions* of channels. Unfortunately, some of us have a tendency to frequently tune into the Anxiety Channel. This channel produces thoughts and images that distress us. Just like some people like to watch news and others prefer to watch reality television, some people seem to get captivated by thoughts that focus on what could go wrong or how other people are likely to react negatively. These thoughts are based on the cortex's ability to *anticipate* what events might occur in the future, even if the cortex has never experienced these events before. This amazing anticipatory ability has only developed in humans, not in other animals, and it's what has allowed us to learn how to plant crops, build airplanes, and design computers. If you are an imaginative, creative person, you are probably very good at anticipating.

Unfortunately, our ability to anticipate also allows us to experience the Anxiety Channel, causing our amygdala to react in response to these distressing thoughts and images in ways that cause us to suffer. Although we could focus instead on all kinds of other channels in the cortex—including the Crossword Puzzle Channel, Plan Your Garden Channel, Talk Politics Channel, Reminisce about Childhood Channel, Gossip about the Family Channel, Plan Your Retirement Channel, or Fantasy Football Channel—some of us spend way too much time on the Anxiety Channel. Of course, if no one has explained to you the relationship between the cortex and the amygdala, you will have no idea that the difference between a calm morning and an anxious morning can depend on what "channel" your cortex is focused on.

If you take a careful look at any negative thoughts you commonly have—like "I won't be good enough," "Things will never go right," or "Everyone is going to judge me"—you may recognize that your cortex is the source of a great deal of amygdala activation. You can change these thoughts, which will require some effort on your part, but it's certainly easier than changing how your amygdala reacts to these thoughts, which is not under your control. Unlike your amygdala, your cortex can learn from logical explanations and plan new coping strategies that make your amygdala less likely to become activated.

How Does the Amygdala Affect the Cortex?

Just as the cortex can affect the amygdala, we also need to remember that the amygdala can affect the thinking processes that occur in the cortex. As we've noted in previous chapters, when the amygdala is producing the defense response, it has the power to direct the cortex's attention to the perceived threat, making it difficult for the cortex to focus on anything else other than the danger the amygdala has alerted it to. This can occur even when no true danger exists (and even when we don't *want* to focus on the potential danger). This is true whether the amygdala was activated via the amygdala pathway or the cortex pathway.

Once the amygdala becomes activated and starts influencing the cortex, our thinking processes may become impaired. We lose control over our thoughts and perceptions, and this increases with the degree of amygdala activation. We may fail to notice or consider important details in our surroundings, and we may have difficulty thinking in an organized, complex, or logical way. We may become overwhelmed by a desire to flee or fight, or we may freeze and be unable to take any action at all. Under these circumstances, we don't have access to the problem-solving or planning abilities in our frontal lobes, so we don't make decisions based on reason. Rather, we are more likely to respond to the emotional and physical reactions the amygdala is creating in our body, which seem to suggest that a true danger or threat exists (even if it does not).

Therefore, it will be difficult to use cognitive coping strategies when the amygdala is strongly activated. The only way to access the problem-solving capabilities in your cortex is to first focus on reducing amygdala activation. This means you need to practice amygdala-calming techniques (such as deep breathing or exercise) and wait for sympathetic activation to decrease. You will be able to use logic and problem solve effectively only *after* the amygdala has calmed down in a way that allows more normal cortex functioning to return.

Making Changes in Your Cortex

Although the amygdala has more influence over the cortex when there is a perceived threat in the environment, the cortex is much more capable of taking charge of your life under normal circumstances. That's because your cortex is able to learn and change from a greater variety of sources than the amygdala: from observation, education (including books like this one), experience, and practice. With sufficient practice, your cortex *can* learn to reduce its tendency to unnecessarily activate the amygdala and provoke the defense response.

Over the years, I have put together guidance on working with the cortex that has proved helpful to my clients in reducing the likelihood of amygdala activation. First of all, you need to learn how to make changes in the thoughts your cortex produces. Unfortunately, one of the first things you will recognize about the cortex is that when you try to *not* think a certain thought, it is very difficult to stop having that thought! For example, if I instruct you right now to not think about your grandmother, a thought or image of your grandmother will immediately pop into your head. That's because our memories are stored in neurons in the brain, which the prefrontal cortex activates in order to access information. So when you read the words "your grandmother," your cortex activates the neurons storing information about your grandmother, which makes it impossible for you to not think about her.

Instead of telling yourself not to think about something (e.g., "Stop constantly focusing on Grandma's heart problems"), you need to replace that thought by telling yourself to think about something else. For example, if I ask you to describe what you want to accomplish in your garden this year, you will find that you have stopped thinking about your grandmother. A good way to remember this approach is to say, "You can't erase; you must *replace*." This approach is effective because the human cortex has the following limitation: Even though it is capable of *doing* many things at once, it cannot *focus* on more than one thing at a time. (That's why you shouldn't text and drive—you cannot focus on the phone and the road at the same time.) This limitation becomes an advantage when you are trying to stop tuning into the Anxiety Channel. Instead of continuing to focus your attention on a certain thought, experience, topic, or memory playing on the Anxiety Channel, you can simply change the channel!

When I encourage you to change the channel, I'm not doing so because those thoughts are dangerous. They are simply thoughts, and they may or may not have any relationship to reality. For example, when Alma thought something had happened to her puppy in the middle of the night, that was simply a thought, and the thought itself was not dangerous. The thought had no effect on the puppy's safety. What made it a problem was the effect it had on Alma's amygdala. Remember, thoughts can activate the amygdala whether or not they are true.

Even if you are having distressing thoughts that *are* true, you may still wish to change these thoughts if they are creating a problem in your life. For example, Kay had to receive monthly eye injections for eight months to treat a problem in her retina, and she felt panicky whenever she thought about her next appointment. In this case, her amygdala had a good reason to be activated: Kay was going to have a needle inserted into her eyeball on a specific date! But should Kay continually focus on this information? What purpose would that serve? If she instead kept her mind off the Eye Injection Channel, then she could prevent herself from experiencing overwhelming anxiety on the 29 days in between appointments. This is not to say that it was easy for Kay to distract herself from upcoming appointments, but when she made a point to keep herself busy and occupy her mind with other thoughts, she had days that were much calmer and more pleasant.

When your goal is to make changes to your thoughts, another important characteristic of the cortex is helpful to know: The cortex is able to access certain thoughts and information more easily than others. In particular, information becomes easier to access when it is used more frequently, which is why the rule of the cortex is "survival of the busiest" (Schwartz & Begley, 2003, p. 117). For example, it is easier to remember the names of people you see often, while it's more difficult to remember the names of people you have not seen for a while. It is the same with other types of thoughts. Thoughts that you have more frequently, especially those that you rehearse over and over again, become easier to bring to mind. The more we obsess and worry about topics, the more we are strengthening those thoughts and making them more likely to occur.

Therefore, when you want to weaken a thought to stop thinking it, the best way to do so is to not use it. The phrase "use it or lose it" definitely applies to thoughts and information in the cortex. Let's return to the example of Nate, who was obsessing about whether his girlfriend would break up with him. When Nate's therapist told him that he needed to stop watching the Breakup Channel, he was doubtful that it would help. In response, his therapist asked if he had ever learned a foreign language, and when he said he had learned some Hebrew, she asked if he could say a couple of sentences in Hebrew. Nate shook his head and said, "I haven't thought about it for so long, I have forgotten it." His therapist replied, "The same thing can happen if you don't constantly think about your girlfriend breaking up with you. Your constant focus on breaking up is only strengthening those kinds of thoughts and doubts." This convinced Nate to explore other channels on which he could focus his attention. Both he and his girlfriend appreciated the difference.

Whenever you realize that you are having amygdala-activating thoughts, keep in mind the rules of "you can't erase; you must replace" and "survival of the busiest." By replacing distressing thoughts with other thoughts, you can change the information coming through the cortex pathway and have a much calmer amygdala (Pittman & Karle, 2015). In the long run, you are also weakening the cortex circuitry holding those specific thoughts and making them less likely to occur. In the next chapter, you will learn to identify the types of thoughts that are most likely to activate the amygdala so you can recognize which thoughts contribute to your own difficulties with anxiety and focus on making your cortex less likely to produce them.

Chapter 12

Identifying Thoughts That Activate the Amygdala

Although we are all perfectly capable of frightening the amygdala with our thoughts and worries, is that necessary or helpful? Do we need to activate the defense response? As you know, very few of the difficulties that we face in our modern lives are solved by fighting, fleeing, or freezing. But those are the amygdala's primitive response patterns, which means that if you want to use more complex processes that involve logic, problem solving, and planning, you need to keep your amygdala from becoming activated and taking charge, using the strategies you learned in chapters 5 through 10. And, as we just discussed in chapter 11, you also need to work to manage the thoughts in your cortex so they don't undermine all your amygdala-calming efforts. In this chapter, you'll learn how to do that with *cognitive restructuring*, which is a method that involves replacing amygdala-activating thoughts with new thought patterns and then practicing those new patterns until they become stronger. This will help you modify your thoughts in a way that makes your overall thinking processes more affirming, calming, and adaptive.

As humans, we learn to interpret situations based on our life experiences, including the interactions we have with our family members, teachers, and peers. These thinking patterns typically carry over from childhood into adulthood, and we're rarely prompted to question whether these patterns might not be serving us well. For example, Amy was an outstanding student who learned quickly and excelled in most of her classes, receiving praise and encouragement for her performance. However, when she tried out for cheerleading, she found it difficult to learn the routines and was embarrassed that she couldn't do so quickly. She had a similar experience when she tried taking a dance class. Amy learned to avoid these kinds of situations because she thought that if she didn't excel at something right away, it was not for her.

Years later, when she was in her 30s, Amy was invited to participate in a folk-dancing group. She enjoyed the experience, but she again found it difficult to learn the dance steps, and her first inclination was to quit. Other group members were constantly giving her suggestions to improve her steps, but she was too embarrassed to try some of the more complicated dances because they looked too challenging. Her cortex was saying, "This is not for me. I'm not good at this." However, the group was such fun and the people were so friendly that Amy didn't want to give up. She realized that the thoughts from her childhood—that she should not engage in activities when she did not excel at them—were leading to anxiety and keeping her from having a good time. This was not a competition, and she didn't have to be an excellent dancer in order to enjoy herself. Amy decided to let go of the thoughts that didn't fit her current life and goals. She embraced being a mediocre folk dancer and had a great time.

Assessing Your Own Patterns of Thinking

Like Amy, you can change thoughts that aren't serving you well or that are blocking you from your goals. But before you can do this, you need to become aware of the underlying thought patterns that you have in the first place. Therefore, in this section, you'll find a series of checklists that will help you to assess your typical patterns of thinking. You may find that you interpret situations in ways that may not make sense or may not be necessary in your current life. Then you can consider and observe how these thoughts affect your life, especially in terms of amygdala activation. Remember that you don't have to bring the amygdala into every situation that stresses you out. You can learn to take back control by reducing the frequency of amygdala-activating thoughts.

Pessimism

One of most common patterns of thinking that increases amygdala activation is **pessimism**. If you tend to expect the worst to happen, you are producing thoughts and images that are likely to activate the amygdala, even before anything distressing has actually occurred. Read through the following statements to gauge the extent to which you engage in pessimistic thinking, checking off those that apply to you.

❏ When someone is late, I often imagine that something has gone wrong.

❏ I often believe that there is no use in trying. Things will never work out for me.

❏ When I want to make a request of someone, I expect that they will say no.

❏ When I need to accomplish something, I frequently expect to have difficulties.

❏ To prepare myself, it is best to expect that something is likely to go wrong.

❏ It is just my luck that things are not going to work out for me.

❏ I often prepare myself for bad things that never happen.

❏ I have found that most people will let you down in the end.

❏ It is hard for me to try because things seem so hopeless.

If you checked off more than three of these statements, you have a tendency toward pessimistic thinking that is likely to activate your amygdala on a regular basis. When you live with the expectation that situations will turn out badly, your amygdala is constantly being exposed to distressing thoughts and images. But you don't have to interpret situations according to these expectations. You can replace these thoughts with **coping thoughts**, which allow you to experience less anxiety and distress. Remember that you can't erase thoughts; you must replace them with other thoughts.

Coping thoughts for pessimism include statements like "I don't know what is going to happen," "Let's wait and see before assuming anything," or "I can handle whatever happens." These thoughts are less likely to activate the amygdala. Even if the situation does turn out badly, you will have reduced the amount of time you had to live with an activated amygdala. Why start suffering before you even experience anything negative?

Anticipation

Another common thought pattern you may experience is **anticipation**, in which you spend a great deal of time thinking about an upcoming event, considering different outcomes, and rehearsing how you could respond. While anticipation can be helpful in planning, it can focus too much time on potential problems and expose the amygdala to distressing images and thoughts that may never be relevant. Anticipation so often feels worse than the anticipated event itself! Check off any of the following statements that apply to you.

- ❏ I frequently find myself considering a problem from a variety of angles.

- ❏ It is difficult to stop myself from thinking about things that make me anxious.

- ❏ I try to have solutions for a variety of outcomes, no matter how unlikely.

- ❏ I need to think about an upcoming situation in detail in order to prepare myself.

- ❏ I frequently prepare responses to criticisms I expect (but don't receive) from others.

- ❏ When an important event is coming up, my thoughts about it interfere with my sleep.

- ❏ I am never sure that I have prepared myself enough for an upcoming event.

- ❏ I know that I dwell on upcoming events, but it seems necessary.

- ❏ When I daydream, it is almost always about negative events, not positive ones.

If you checked off more than three of these statements, you may be overusing anticipation and producing more amygdala activation than is necessary. You may benefit from coping statements like "I have thought about this enough, and I will get through it" or "I can figure out what to do once I'm in the situation." Another way to replace anticipatory thoughts is to keep yourself engaged with other situations, activities, or topics that have a present-moment focus. This helps ground you to what is happening *right now* so you can stop thinking so much about the future. Engage in activities that are entertaining so you can enjoy each day as you experience it.

Mind Reading

Some people spend a great deal of time trying to figure out what other people are thinking in the hopes that they can please others or manage their reactions. While it is important to be considerate of what others might be thinking, it's easy to go too far and make assumptions that are based more on our own worries. This type of **mind reading** can increase amygdala activation because it focuses your attention on critical or negative thoughts that others *may* have about you or about something that concerns you. When you spend time trying to determine what is happening in another person's mind, you often make incorrect assumptions in the absence of any real evidence. To determine how much you may be mind reading, consider if any of the following statements apply to you.

❏ I often hear other people's criticisms of me in my mind, even when they've said nothing.

❏ I frequently prepare responses to people's statements before they have spoken.

❏ I expect others to have a negative view of me and am surprised by compliments.

❏ I frequently get the sense that I am a disappointment to others.

❏ I often assume that others are irritated with me, even when they deny it.

❏ I want to be prepared to defend myself against other people's opinions of me.

❏ I hesitate to ask for anything from others because I expect rejection.

❏ When I hear that someone is upset, I tend to assume I have something to do with it.

❏ I often don't believe what other people tell me they think, especially about me.

If you checked off more than three of these statements, your tendency to engage in mind reading may be leading to unnecessary amygdala activation. Humans are social creatures, so we are often very concerned with the possibility of others criticizing or rejecting us. However, when there is no evidence to suggest that someone else has negative thoughts about you, you could benefit from replacing mind-reading thoughts with thoughts like "I can't know what they are thinking without discussing it with them" and "I can't please everyone, and it is not my job to do so anyway." You can also ask yourself, "Did the other person really say that, or am I just assuming?"

It is most beneficial to make decisions based on your own feelings, experiences, and judgments rather than constantly trying to figure out what others think. Sometimes we worry too much about pleasing others, even people we barely know or may never see again! Although there are some people we need to be concerned about, like our work supervisors or family members, it is really unnecessary (and impossible) to be liked and approved of by everyone. It's not always worth it to worry about what others think. Many of your guesses will activate the amygdala, even when your assumptions are incorrect or when the person's opinion will have little impact on your life.

Catastrophizing

Another pattern of thinking that can activate the amygdala is **catastrophizing**, which involves responding to a small setback or minor difficulty as if it is a catastrophe. When our expectations are not met or when something goes wrong, it makes sense to feel frustrated or disappointed, but it doesn't mean our whole day has to be ruined. If you have ever lost your temper when you've been stopped by a red light, or completely panicked when you couldn't find your keys for several minutes, you have catastrophized. Catastrophic thoughts like "I'm going to be late and be seen as incompetent!" or "I won't be able to drive my car all day!" are just the kind to activate the amygdala because they present the situation as one that is very threatening. Consider the following statements to see if you have a tendency to catastrophize.

❐ When something goes wrong, I tend to imagine the worst possible outcome.

❐ I tend to overreact to small setbacks.

❐ I often feel like giving up when I hit a snag in something I am working on.

❐ When something breaks, I have a tendency to see it as disastrous.

❐ I often feel like I can't cope with even one thing going wrong.

❐ I frequently get infuriated when someone makes a mistake that affects me.

❐ I admit that I can often make a mountain out of a molehill.

❐ I notice that other people interpret problems more calmly than I do.

❐ People have told me that I overreact to minor difficulties.

If you checked more than three of these statements, you most likely have a tendency to catastrophize. To calm your amygdala, try replacing catastrophic thinking with more realistic thoughts, like "Getting stuck at this traffic light will only make me arrive a minute later, and I can handle that" or "This is not the worst thing that could happen." The next time you encounter a difficulty that makes you want to catastrophize, take a breath and give yourself a few moments to adjust. Try not to jump to the conclusion that all is lost when you could be more hopeful about what the rest of the day will bring.

Perfectionistic Thinking

Although you might not realize it, **perfectionistic thinking** also activates our amygdala and puts us in a constant state of fear: the fear of being imperfect. When we hold ourselves to perfectionistic standards, the amygdala learns to respond to mistakes and imperfections as threatening. However, no one is perfect, so perfectionism creates a standard that is impossible to achieve. We will all inevitably fail, mess up, or have setbacks at times, and the immense self-criticism and disappointment that result from perfectionism create a sense of danger in our amygdala. Look over the following statements to consider whether you have a tendency toward perfectionistic thoughts.

❐ I have a great deal of difficulty admitting or accepting my mistakes.

❐ I believe there is a best way to do things, and I don't want to compromise.

❐ I try to hold myself to very high standards.

❐ It's important to expect a lot of myself and not allow any excuses.

❏ I want to be a careful, conscientious, and hard worker every day.

❏ I expect myself to be a high achiever in everything I undertake.

❏ I rarely am satisfied with my performance.

❏ It is hard to forgive myself for errors. Even minor ones haunt me.

❏ I expect myself to perform better than others in most situations.

If you checked off more than three of these statements, your amygdala is likely experiencing frequent activation because every day presents you with the likelihood that you will not live up to your perfectionistic standards. Many of us have been raised to believe that we should always do our best, and we may equate that with perfectionism, which is an exhausting and unreasonable ideal. Often, perfectionism involves the constant need to outshine others, do everything correctly, and know more than others. It comes with the expectation of complete and utter flawlessness from a normal, imperfect individual, which is simply unsustainable. The reality is that we all have strengths and weaknesses. Further, we don't *always* need to do our best. If you were to give 100 percent when performing every single task (e.g., brushing your teeth, making your bed, preparing breakfast), you would be exhausted from the constant pressure by the end of the day. It's healthier to choose what to do your best at.

Perhaps the most obvious coping statement to replace perfectionistic thoughts is the simple reminder that "no one is perfect." When you catch yourself criticizing your imperfections or mistakes, let yourself off the hook and say, "I have talents and skills, but I can't be perfect." It is healthy to see mistakes and imperfections as a normal part of being human.

Cognitive Fusion

When we take our thoughts too seriously—becoming so "fused" with them that it's hard to disentangle them from reality—we are experiencing **cognitive fusion**. We worry that simply thinking about something means that it will definitely happen, either through our own or others' actions. For example, someone might have the thought that their partner is cheating on them, and then believe that having this worry makes it true. However, it is actually very common for people to have random thoughts pop into their minds, and overestimating the importance of those thoughts is the source of the problem. For instance, someone who has intrusive thoughts about how deadly it would be to drive in front of a semitruck on the highway may be surprised to learn that most people experience thoughts like this—and having these thoughts does not mean they are in danger of killing themselves. Here are some statements to help you determine whether you experience cognitive fusion.

❏ When I have a worry, I often think that my worry is very likely to come true.

❏ I take my anxiety to be a clear indication that something is going to go wrong.

❏ Some of my thoughts truly frighten me.

❏ I often worry that I may act on thoughts that I have, even though I don't want to.

❐ When I think something will go wrong, it usually means that it will.

❐ I worry about what certain thoughts mean and what I will do as a result of them.

❐ If I think I can't do something, I know it's best to just give up.

❐ When images come into my mind, I can't help but think they will come true.

❐ I think it is important to take my thoughts very seriously.

If you checked off more than three of these items, you may have a tendency to overvalue your thoughts. This means your amygdala is prone to react when there is no evidence of danger. To cope with the effects of cognitive fusion, remember not to accept thoughts without verification. Instead of taking them at face value, ask yourself, "What evidence supports this thought?" Remind yourself that simply having a thought doesn't mean that it will come true. Label your thoughts as only thoughts—for example: "I'm having the thought that I'm going to fail, but that doesn't mean I will." Try to be observant of your thoughts and approach them with a healthy skepticism: "Although I'm aware of this pesky thought, I have no reason to put faith in it" or "This is the kind of thought that activates my amygdala." Remind yourself that these thoughts have been wrong in the past.

Shoulds

The way you approach goals for yourself can also affect amygdala activation. When you frame your goals as **shoulds**, you are putting pressure on yourself that is not necessary for change to occur. These should statements can come in the form of thoughts about the need to behave in a correct way ("I *should* always be patient with my child and never lose my temper.") or be a better person ("I *should* be more organized."). Feelings of guilt often result from should statements focused on specific behaviors, whereas feelings of shame result from should statements focused on the sense of being flawed as a person.

Because these statements increase guilt and shame, they typically increase distress rather than supporting the change process. If the should statement is focused on something a person did that was objectively wrong ("I *should* not have said hurtful things to my friend in the heat of the argument"), the ensuing guilt can be helpful in encouraging the person to seek forgiveness, correct the behavior, and make a commitment to not repeat it. But guilt can be unhealthy when it comes from should statements that impart unrealistic self-blame or rigid, high standards. And should statements that cause shame are never healthy, as they simply make you believe that you are worthless or hopelessly flawed, while offering no clear way to resolve the situation or feel more positively about yourself. Consider the following statements to see if you have a tendency to "should" yourself.

❐ I know I should be a better person.

❐ I frequently tell myself what I should do or how I should be.

❐ While I don't necessarily say "I should…" out loud, I frequently think it to myself.

❐ I beat myself up when I've hurt someone's feelings.

❑ I have high expectations for myself.

❑ When I set a goal for myself, I can be very hard on myself.

❑ I tend to be harder on myself than on other people.

❑ I hate it when I feel like I've let someone down.

❑ It is difficult for me to tell someone no.

❑ I often suspect that others are disappointed with me.

❑ If someone wants something, it's easy for them to guilt me into doing it for them.

❑ I feel ashamed about who I have become.

If you checked off more than three of these statements, your amygdala is likely to be frequently activated by should statements, which can make it feel like you are not measuring up to some standard. However, it's important to ask yourself where this standard came from. Oftentimes, we set unreasonable expectations for ourselves that only serve to perpetuate anxiety, guilt, and shame. While it is true that expectations can motivate you to improve yourself and your relationships with others, when you are constantly "shoulding" yourself, you are holding on to guilt and shame that will activate the amygdala and increase your suffering. If you are stuck in this cycle, you first need to consider whether you believe that you deserve to suffer from the distress that the amygdala is creating. Part of you may believe it would be wrong to stop suffering. But do guilt and shame lead to beneficial results for you and others, or are you stuck in a useless cycle of suffering?

One way to overcome self-critical should statements is to replace "I should" with a preference statement, such as "I want to," "I would prefer it if," or "I would like to." These statements are less emotionally charged and don't get you stuck in the same cycle of anxiety, guilt, disappointment, frustration, and shame. For example, instead of berating yourself by saying "I should exercise more," see what it's like to use a preference statement instead: "I would like to exercise more."

In addition, if you find that you are "shoulding" yourself in response to some healthy standard—for example, perhaps you didn't treat someone as kindly as you would have liked to—you can benefit from making reparations and then practicing thoughts that focus on the present and future: "The best thing I can do is commit myself to engaging in better behaviors today and in the future" or "Guilt and shame keep me focused on the past. What do I want to do *today* that makes a difference in someone's life?" You can also work to let go of the guilt and shame by replacing should statements with coping statements, such as "When I acted that way, I did not intend to create the harm I did" or "I was not the only cause of the situation; other people's decisions and actions played a role too."

Distressing Images

It's not only certain thought patterns that can activate your amygdala. Some people also have a tendency to visualize threatening or **distressing images** that produce a strong defense response. In fact, the amygdala may respond more strongly to negative images than it does to thoughts or worries (Freeston et al., 1996). Remember, the amygdala often responds to thoughts of threatening situations as if it were being exposed to the actual situation, and visual images provoke the strongest response. Our capacity for visual imagery comes from the right hemisphere, so if you have a creative imagination and can visualize a variety of events and scenes, you are probably very capable of using images to activate the amygdala. Read the following statements to see if distressing images are a common way you activate your amygdala.

- ❏ I often imagine myself acting in a way that would be embarrassing.

- ❏ I sometimes see horrific images when I am worrying about something.

- ❏ I can't help but imagine scenes in which someone I care about is injured or ill.

- ❏ I frequently visualize terrible events that I worry will occur.

- ❏ Even when I am awake, I experience images that are like nightmares.

- ❏ It is very easy for me to produce a distressing scenario in my mind.

- ❏ It is very natural to imagine myself in embarrassing situations.

- ❏ Other people would be shocked at the images that sometimes appear in my mind.

- ❏ I'm more likely to imagine myself in a situation than to make a plan to cope with it.

If you checked off more than three of these responses, distressing imagery is likely keeping your amygdala activated. To keep yourself from producing these images, try replacing the distressing scene with a positive one by deliberately visualizing yourself in a positive or relaxing situation. Or you can use coping thoughts from the left hemisphere to manage the situation, such as "Don't imagine anything when you have no evidence for it—it only produces stress" or "Find something useful to focus yourself on. These images have no benefits." You can also use distraction by focusing on another task or watching a television show that focuses you on other images.

Tracking Amygdala-Activating Thoughts

You've just explored a variety of thinking patterns that can trigger the defense response even when you are not in a truly dangerous situation. Now it is time to look into your own life to identify situations that provoke the defense response and to consider how your thoughts about those situations could be activating your amygdala. Use the following worksheet to explore how your cortex can activate the amygdala simply by the way it interprets certain situations.

Tracking Amygdala-Activating Thoughts

Start by choosing a situation in which you tend to experience feelings of anxiety or distress associated with the defense response. It's especially helpful to choose a situation that relates to the goals you identified in chapter 3. Then follow these steps:

1. In the first column of the chart (**Situation**), briefly describe the situation you chose to focus on.

2. Skip to the third column (**Signs of Amygdala Activation**), and describe how your amygdala tends to react in this situation by writing down any sensations, emotions, or impulses you typically experience. It might be helpful to review your answers to the prompts in chapter 5, as well as the notes you made in the **Indicators of the Defense Response** worksheet.

3. Now focus on the second column (**Interpretations That Lead to Amygdala Activation**). Write down any thoughts that your cortex produces in this situation that you suspect might lead to amygdala activation. Remember to consider your own tendencies toward certain patterns of thinking: pessimism, anticipation, mind reading, catastrophizing, perfectionistic thinking, cognitive fusion, shoulds, or distressing images.

4. Finally, at the bottom of the chart, identify what the amygdala fears will happen as a result of these interpretations. Consider what message the amygdala is getting from the cortex. Are *you* overestimating the danger in the situation along with the amygdala?

    On the next page is an example of a completed chart, followed by a blank one for you to use on your own.

Situation	Interpretations That Lead to Amygdala Activation	Signs of Amygdala Activation
Going to the public library	• They'll think I am uneducated. • I will seem stupid. • I'm feeling ashamed of my dyslexia. • The library makes me think of things I'm not good at.	• Trembling • Nervous • Nauseous • Wanting to leave • Unable to think clearly

Because of my thoughts, in this situation, my amygdala reacts as if the following danger will occur:

• The librarians will criticize me or make fun of me.

• Everyone will know I have dyslexia.

• I am going to fail at something.

Don't scare your amygdala!

Situation	Interpretations That Lead to Amygdala Activation	Signs of Amygdala Activation

Because of my thoughts, in this situation, my amygdala reacts as if the following danger will occur:

Don't scare your amygdala!

The previous worksheet prompts you to consider whether your cortex's interpretations are helping you or leading to problems. For example, Jackie realized that she was mind reading when she thought she knew what the librarians were thinking. She had no evidence that they would judge her harshly or figure out that she had dyslexia. She realized how much those thoughts were scaring her amygdala, and she worked to replace them with coping thoughts, like "Give the librarians a chance" and "Don't be scared of a librarian." She also reminded herself that "dyslexia is nothing to be ashamed of" and encouraged herself by saying, "Going to the library is a goal of mine, and it will help me be more educated." She found that with these thoughts in her mind, she was able to stop avoiding the library—and she was relieved to find how welcoming and helpful the librarians were.

Combating Amygdala-Activating Thoughts

If you find that you need additional tools to combat amygdala-activating thoughts, the following worksheet can be helpful, especially if these thoughts are discouraging you or interfering with your ability to do exposures. When you have minimal evidence to support your cortex's interpretations, you may find these tools especially effective in helping you to question your amygdala-activating thoughts and to replace them with more useful coping thoughts. The prompts in the worksheet encourage you to use logic and reasoning to make sure your thoughts aren't activating the amygdala when you are trying to teach it that the situation is safe. A completed example is provided for you first, followed by a blank template for you to use on your own.

Combating Amygdala-Activating Thoughts

To get into the habit of challenging your amygdala-activating thoughts, read through the following example, which takes you through the steps involved in modifying a distressing thought and replacing it with a more useful coping thought. Then practice applying the steps to an amygdala-activating thought of your own using the blank template on the next page.

Amygdala-activating thought	When I attend the church potluck, I'll say something that will make people laugh at or criticize me.
Has this ever happened? How many times? What was the situation?	This has happened, but not at church. Several times I was laughed at and criticized in a group setting like this. That was in high school.
Evidence that this is (or is not) likely to occur	The people at church tend to be kind with me and with one another. I chose this location for this step because I know that.
Actual chance of this happening (0%–100%)	I think I can be cautious about what I say, and because they are kind, the probability is only about 5%–10%.
How to cope	If someone does laugh or criticize, I can laugh along at myself or I can listen to them and say, "That's a good point."
Coping thought	I don't have to be perfect, and I can handle possible criticism. I just need to stay there and get through it and I'll have succeeded.

Amygdala-activating thought	
Has this ever happened? How many times? What was the situation?	
Evidence that this is (or is not) likely to occur	
Actual chance of this happening (0%–100%)	
How to cope	
Coping thought	

Now that you know how the amygdala monitors and responds to what occurs in the cortex, you can understand the importance of what you think. You have learned that certain thoughts can activate the amygdala, and you have already identified some of these thoughts in your own cortex. These thoughts may not reflect reality, but they can definitely scare the amygdala! However, by continuing to practice recognizing these thoughts and replacing them with more useful coping thoughts, you are taming your amygdala.

Chapter 13

How to Use Worry Correctly

Understanding worry is crucial in taming your amygdala. Worry is the process of thinking about the potential negative outcomes of a situation before they have happened. It involves focusing on negative events that could occur, problems that could develop, and situations that could harm or embarrass you. Worry largely arises in the orbitofrontal cortex, which is a part of our frontal lobes located behind our eyes. This part of the brain helps us consider various outcomes (both good and bad) that could occur in a situation (Grupe & Nitschke, 2013). We can even worry about something that we have never seen before because we have very creative and imaginative cortexes. This ability to anticipate what might happen and even to visualize it in detail is specific to humans; you need the unique capabilities of the human cortex to be able to worry.

In this chapter, you will learn about the roots of worry in our history as humans and the foundations of worry in the brain. You will also learn how to use worry in a way that is beneficial, as well as how to keep worry from activating your amygdala and leading to a pattern of anxiety that takes over your life. Worry can sustain anxiety and distress for days if you don't understand how to use it correctly, but with the right tools you can harness its power.

The Evolution of Worry

Let's start at the beginning by going back to prehistoric times. Our ancestors did not always have worry circuitry in their cortexes, but as their frontal lobes developed—getting larger and more complicated—ancient humans acquired the ability to anticipate, a distinctly human trait that has adaptive benefits (Grupe et al., 2013). For example, humans learned to predict when the weather would turn cold and what situations would occur as a result of this change (e.g., their water would freeze and their shelters would become inadequate). To some extent, humans developed this ability by using their memory of past experiences to form expectations about the future. But what's even more impressive is that they developed the ability to imagine events they had never experienced before. By taking advantage of the frontal lobe's planning circuits, humans were able to plan and execute amazing activities, like planting food, creating clothing, and building bridges. These abilities to anticipate, imagine, and plan have led to many amazing human achievements. But we are getting ahead of the story…

Here's an example that illustrates how worry circuits could have developed as a useful ability in our species. Imagine a prehistoric woman who has built a little hut near a stream, which she thinks is good location. She has easy access to water and fish, and all seems well. But one day, when torrential rain falls, the woman sees the stream growing higher. Because this woman has worry circuits in her brain, she can imagine the stream growing so large that it washes her hut away. This image activates the woman's amygdala, resulting in the defense response and creating accompanying anxiety and distress. But because she can plan, this woman builds a new hut farther away from the stream, where she and her family can move to be safe. If she hadn't had the worry circuitry to imagine this potential danger, she and her family may not have survived if a flood had occurred.

As this story suggests, the ability to worry can have an evolutionary advantage. That's why modern humans are likely to be descendants of the worried people: Those who worried about potential threats were more likely to survive than those who were not worriers. It is no wonder that so many of us seem to have inherited the ability to be excellent worriers! But if you consider the story more closely, you will realize that worrying alone was not what helped the woman. If she had *only* worried, that would not have helped her and her family. She would have felt distressed, but nothing would have changed. It was her ability to *plan* that made the real difference. Because she came up with a plan and took action, she and her family were more likely to survive.

Therefore, if you have a tendency to worry, it will only be beneficial to you if you know how to use that worry correctly. Worry alerts you to a potential problem, but it doesn't solve the problem unless you come up with a plan. Once you make a plan and take action, worry has served its purpose and is no longer needed. Unfortunately, most people who worry do not understand how to use worry in the most beneficial way, so they end up getting stuck in their worry and distress and then suffer needlessly from an activated amygdala.

Assessing Your Worry

Would you consider yourself a worrier? Usually worriers are aware of their worrying because they realize that they are often deliberately thinking about things that could go wrong. But if you're unsure whether you are a worrier, read through these statements and check off any that you think are true of you.

- ❏ I frequently think about things that could go wrong.

- ❏ Whenever I am planning an event, I always think about what problems could occur.

- ❏ When things are going smoothly, I still think of problems that could arise.

- ❏ I have a tendency to anticipate the worst.

- ❏ I know I worry a lot, but I can't help it.

- ❏ My worries overwhelm me at times, and I can't focus on other things.

❏ I can always find something to worry about.

❏ Although many situations make me worry, they often turn out fine.

❏ As soon as I finish one thing, I start to worry about what else I have to do.

If you checked off more than three of these statements, your frequent worries are likely maintaining a constant level of amygdala activation in your life, even when no present danger exists. Ironically, when you analyze the situation in detail, this relieves some of your anxiety because the process of analyzing distracts you from more distressing images and concerns that are most activating to your amygdala (Compton et al., 2008). In the big picture, however, worry-focused thoughts are likely to sustain activation in the amygdala and keep you from relaxing and feeling calm. That's because when you continue to focus on a negative event (whether or not it occurs), you lengthen your emotional reaction, maintaining negative emotions longer than they would have otherwise lasted (Verduyn et al., 2011). You also strengthen the cortex circuitry underlying the worries, making them more likely to be activated, when you want to weaken that circuitry.

One of the challenges in reducing worry is that so many people believe their worry is helpful or protective in some way. Once, when I was working with a client who admitted to being a constant worrier for years, I encouraged her to reduce her worrying about her children (who were now in their 30s and 40s). She said she was reluctant to even try, explaining, "All these years I have worried, and nothing has happened. If I stop worrying, how do I know they will be safe?" You may have a similar tendency to believe that worrying itself could be protective. See how much you agree with each of the following statements.

❏ To be honest, I feel better if I worry.

❏ Once I start worrying, it seems necessary to continue.

❏ If I don't worry, I think my worries are more likely to come true.

❏ Even when there is nothing I can do about a situation, I still worry.

❏ Even when things are going well, I find that worrying still seems helpful.

❏ I believe that my worries have been helpful to me.

❏ When I worry, I somehow feel safer.

❏ I feel like my worrying has protected me or my loved ones.

❏ Worrying is a great relief to me.

If you checked off more than three of these statements, you likely believe that worrying is more helpful than harmful. When people believe that their worries can keep bad things from happening, this is a form of cognitive fusion. They may mistakenly believe that when they worry, nothing seems to go wrong. However, this belief more likely reflects the fact that what they feared was not likely to happen in the first place! Worries have to do with situations that *could* occur, but few of them do. Therefore, instead of helping, frequent worrying only results in a variety of physical and emotional consequences. In fact, worriers have a great deal of difficulty feeling relaxed and at ease, and they may even suffer from high blood pressure and other cardiac effects (Tully et al., 2013; Verkuil et al., 2009) or digestive problems (Renna et al., 2021).

Remember, the benefit of worrying is not the worrying itself; it's the way that worrying (and the sting of amygdala activation) brings a potential concern to our attention, giving us the opportunity to make a plan to cope with this potential difficulty. Worries themselves are not solutions. You can imagine negative outcomes all day, without ever developing a plan to address the situation—and without a plan, worry loses its benefit. Therefore, you'll want to make sure you're using worry correctly.

Getting Your Worries Under Control

The first step in making your worries work *for* you, rather than against you, is to become aware that you are worrying. We often worry without even being conscious of it. As soon as you realize that you are worrying about something, remind yourself to worry in the manner that is most likely to help. Worry subjects you to the stress of amygdala activation, so you want it to be worth the cost. Then, identify what your specific concern is and limit the time you spend worrying about it by shifting your focus to putting a plan in place. For example, if Sam is worried that he forgot to pay his utility bill, he should specify his primary concern (i.e., that the bill has not been paid), and move on from his worry by forming a plan (e.g., checking his bank account or calling the electric company to determine whether the bill is outstanding and, if so, making a payment on it).

You can use the process in figure 14 as a guide. In the box at the top of the figure, the first arrow alerts you to the need to move away from worry and into a plan that will help you prevent, correct, or cope with the situation. The second arrow reminds you to move on with your day once you have a plan in place. You do not need to hold on to worry thoughts; you can focus on other things and live your life.

However, worries are often complicated and do not always have clear solutions. If your worry involves a degree of uncertainty, and you're wondering if a plan is appropriate, the answer is yes! You can still develop a plan to use if needed, even though you may not carry it out. For example, Helen was having a neighborhood barbeque and was worried about the behavior of her neighbor, Stanley, who often drank too much and became obnoxious. Helen wasn't sure Stanley was coming, and she wasn't even sure he would become intoxicated, but she kept imagining distressing scenarios that could occur in her backyard. Helen talked with her husband, Neil, and together they decided that if Stanley came, Neil would keep an eye on him and gently escort him home as soon as possible if any trouble arose. Having a plan in place allowed Helen to let go of her worry and focus on preparing and enjoying the upcoming barbeque. They didn't know whether they would need to use the plan, but simply having it allowed Helen to move on.

In figure 14, you'll notice two other common, but counterproductive, ways that people use worry. The second box in the figure illustrates that some people mistakenly believe they should go back to worrying once they put a plan in place. However, returning to worry is not necessary or helpful; it will only lead to pointless amygdala activation.

You have already formed a plan to deal with the potential problem (which might not even happen). Remember that the second arrow tells you to move on even if you have not executed your plan but are simply keeping it in mind in case it is needed. If you find yourself returning to worry, remind yourself, "I have a plan to deal with this"—and move on.

Figure 14

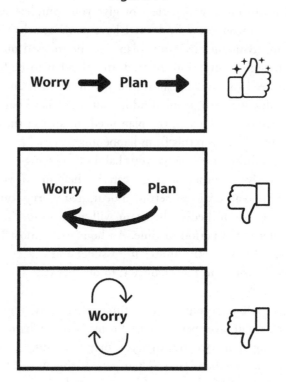

Many of my clients who have a pattern of worry will ask me questions like "What if you are worried about the plan? What if you think the plan will not work? What if there is a flaw in the plan?" You should recognize these thoughts as worries about the plan. And since the best way to deal with worry is to come up with a plan, you may need to modify the plan or come up with a backup plan if you have doubts about the original plan. However, once you come up with that alternative, you need to move on. Continually tinkering with the plan is being stuck in the worry cycle. You just need *a* plan, not a perfect plan. You don't need to be 100 percent confident that it will work. It just needs to give you a sense that you can deal with the situation if it occurs. Then move on with your day.

Finally, the third box in figure 14 illustrates the tendency that many people have to cycle through worry after worry, coming up with distressing scenarios but never changing their focus to making a plan. Therefore, nothing is being accomplished to help the situation. Remember that worry by itself has little benefit. As anxiety expert Reid Wilson wisely wrote, "Worry is supposed to be only a trigger for problem solving. It is not supposed to last a long time" (Wilson, 2016, p. 51). Without a plan, worry does not have a useful result—you just cause yourself to experience undue tension and distress. Don't keep repeatedly subjecting your amygdala to distressing thoughts with no benefit. Remind yourself to move from worry to making a plan, and then move on.

One word of warning about a particular type of worry: Sometimes the things we worry about are normal aspects of life that we need to accept as beyond our control. If your worry is about doing something imperfectly or not knowing (or not being able to control) what will happen in a situation, that is a worry that no amount of problem solving will address. No plan can make you perfect or give you complete certainty or control in life. For worries like "Someone may find out I have panic attacks" or "I won't be able to prevent my wife from divorcing me," your plan can't be focused on keeping those things from happening or fixing the situation. Instead, the plan has to be focused on developing *coping strategies.* You need to strategize how you will respond if and when the worrisome situation occurs: "I will cope with people finding out that I have panic attacks by…" or "I will cope with a divorce by…" That is, the plan needs to answer the question "How will I cope?" rather than "How do I keep this from happening?"

If you're finding it difficult to change your habit of worrying—to worry constructively rather than unnecessarily—another strategy can be helpful. If you have a hard time reducing your worry, you can begin by setting a dedicated **worry time**. Schedule a specific time each day (but not before bed!) when you will allow yourself to worry as much as you'd like for a predetermined period of time. An hour is the most I would allow, and I'd recommend that you keep it to 30 minutes if possible. You can even schedule more than one worry time to begin with and then reduce it to one per day. Then tune into the Worry Channel and worry away!

If you catch yourself worrying at other times of the day, remind yourself, "This is not the time to worry. I will save these worries for my Worry Channel time at 2 p.m." You can also briefly write down any worries that you may have outside of your set worry time so you remember to address them later. Then get off the Worry Channel and focus on other thoughts or activities. In fact, distraction is one of the best ways to change the Worry Channel. By occupying yourself with specific, engaging tasks—such as hobbies, exercise, entertainment, or even work—you'll find that you have less time to worry.

This strategy can help you gain more control over your worrying so you can turn it on and off more effectively. However, you don't need to maintain scheduled worry time forever. Eventually, you can return to less structured worrying, at which time you'll hopefully have greater control over your ability to change the channel to other kinds of thoughts and activities. Sometimes the most difficult part is allowing yourself to focus on something other than your worries. Give yourself permission to try something different! And once you're able to shift your attention away from worries, you may be surprised how much calmer your amygdala can be. You may also be surprised at how much more energy you have when you are not cycling though the process of worry thoughts and amygdala activation. Worry can be exhausting!

Hopefully, this chapter has given you a new way to see your tendency to worry. I hope you recognize that when your cortex is tuned into the Worry Channel, it does not help you to tame your amygdala, and it won't help you accomplish anything *unless* you use your worry correctly by incorporating a plan. Once you have a plan, make sure you move on with your day and focus on other things (remember that you can return to your worries at a scheduled time if needed). Worry can be reduced with exercise, deep breathing, and distraction, even when the situation you are worrying about has not been resolved. So don't assume that worry is the only way to try to find relief.

Conclusion

Taking Back Your Life

Congratulations! You've accomplished a great deal throughout this workbook. You now have a better understanding of how your brain produces fear, anxiety, panic, and worry. You have learned about the two neural pathways to anxiety—and the central role the amygdala plays in each. Now you are prepared to move forward in achieving the goals you've selected for yourself and to not allow the amygdala to stop you from living the life you want.

Although overcoming the amygdala's influence is not easy, you *can* tame your amygdala and put yourself back in the driver's seat. You have learned strategies to help you calm your amygdala, like getting enough sleep, exercising regularly, and practicing relaxation. Further, you now recognize that you do not need to take the protective reactions of the amygdala seriously. Rather than allowing fear, anxiety, and worry to control your life, you can push through these experiences with a determination to reach your goals, recognizing that the primitive fight, flight, and freeze responses are not always helpful in our modern world. Remember, when you allow the amygdala to decide what is best for you—following its urging to avoid, retreat, and seek a feeling of safety—your life can become restricted and unproductive.

Courage is not the absence of fear; it is taking action in spite of fear. With your new understanding of the way the amygdala operates, you can observe what is happening in your body and accept it as a normal process, knowing that it will pass. You understand how to use the exposure process to reduce your amygdala's reaction to triggers, as well as how to change your cortex's patterns of thinking and worrying to keep your amygdala from becoming activated as often. You can teach your amygdala that it can back off and stop being overprotective so you can live your life.

Above all, let the serenity prayer be your guide: Know what you can change about your amygdala and accept what you cannot change. Although some aspects of the defense response are not under your control, you've learned that your life does not need to be anxiety-free in order for you to achieve your goals. With the tools and courage to take charge of your life, you *can* make changes that make your life more satisfying and enjoyable. My hope is that you'll pursue your goals with both determination and playfulness, cherishing the life you create.

References

For your convenience, you may download a PDF version of the worksheets
in this book from our dedicated website: pesi.com/amygdala

al'Absi, M., & Lovallo, W. R. (2004). Caffeine's effects on the human stress axis. In A. Nehlig (Ed.), *Coffee, tea, chocolate, and the brain* (pp. 114–132). CRC Press.

Altena, E., Micoulaud-Franchi, J.-A., Geoffroy, P.-A., Sanz-Arigita, E., Bioulac, S., & Phillip, P. (2016). The bidirectional relation between emotional reactivity and sleep: From disruption to recovery. *Behavioral Neuroscience, 130*(3), 336–350. https://doi.apa.org/doi/10.1037/bne0000128

Anderson, E., & Shivakumar, G. (2013). Effects of exercise and physical activity on anxiety. *Frontiers in Psychiatry, 4*, Article 27. https://doi.org/10.3389/fpsyt.2013.00027

Ashok, I., Wankhar, D., Wankhar, W., & Sheeladevi, R. (2015). Neurobehavioral changes and activation of neurodegenerative apoptosis on long-term consumption of aspartame in the rat brain. *Journal of Nutrition & Intermediary Metabolism, 2*, 76–85. https://doi.org/10.1016/j.jnim.2015.09.001

Atkinson, F. S., Foster-Powell, K., & Brand-Miller, J. C. (2008). International tables of glycemic index and glycemic load values: 2008. *Diabetes Care, 31*(12), 2281–2283. https://dx.doi.org/10.2337%2Fdc08-1239

Babson, K. A., Feldner, M. T., Trainor, C. D., & Smith, R. C. (2009). An experimental investigation of the effects of acute sleep deprivation on panic-relevant biological challenge responding. *Behavior Therapy, 40*(3), 239–250. https://doi.org/10.2337/dc08-1239

Beck, A. T. (1976). *Cognitive therapy and the emotional disorders*. Penguin.

Bernstein, E. E., Curtiss, J. E., Wu, G. W. Y., Barreira, P. J., & McNally, R. J. (2019). Exercise and emotion dynamics: An experience sampling study. *Emotion, 19*(4), 637–644. https://doi.org/10.1037/emo0000462

Bourne, E. J., Brownstein, A., & Garano, L. (2004). *Natural relief for anxiety: Complementary strategies for easing fear, panic, and worry*. New Harbinger.

Brice, C. F., & Smith, A. P. (2002). Effects of caffeine on mood and performance: A study of realistic consumption. *Psychopharmacology, 164*(2), 188–192. https://doi.org/10.1007/s00213-002-1175-2

Cacciaglia, R., Nees, F. Grimm, O., Ridder, S., Pohlack, S. T. Diener, S. J., Liebscher, C., & Flor, H. (2017). Trauma exposure relates to heightened stress, altered amygdala morphology and deficient extinction learning: Implications for psychopathology. *Psychoneuroendocrinology, 76,* 19–28. https://doi.org/10.1016/j.psyneuen.2016.11.012

Cahill, S. P., Franklin, M. E., & Feeny, N. C. (2006). Pathological anxiety: Where we are and where we need to go. In B. O. Rothbaum (Ed.), *Pathological anxiety: Emotional processing in etiology and treatment* (pp. 245–265). Guilford Press.

Carskadon, M. A., & Dement, W. C. (2011). Monitoring and staging human sleep. In M. H. Kryger, T. Roth, & W. C. Dement (Eds.), *Principles and practice of sleep medicine* (5th ed., pp. 16–26). Saunders.

Chan, J. K. M., Trinder, J., Andrewes, H. E., Colrain, I. M., & Nicholas, C. L. (2013). The acute effects of alcohol on sleep architecture in late adolescence. *Alcoholism: Clinical and Experimental Research, 37*(10), 1720–1728. https://doi.org/10.1111/acer.12141

Chang, A.-M., Aeschbach, D., Duffy, J. F., & Czeisler, C. A. (2015). Evening use of light-emitting eReaders negatively affects sleep, circadian timing, and next-morning alertness. *PNAS, 112*(4), 1232–1237. https://doi.org/10.1073/pnas.1418490112

Chen, Y.-C., Chen, C., Martínez, R. M., Etnier, J. L., & Cheng, Y. (2019). Habitual physical activity mediates the acute exercise-induced modulation of anxiety-related amygdala functional connectivity. *Scientific Reports, 9,* Article 19787. https://doi.org/10.1038/s41598-019-56226-z

Childs, E., Hohoff, C., Deckert, J., Xu, K., Badner, J., & de Wit, H. (2008). Association between ADORA2A and DRD2 polymorphisms and caffeine-induced anxiety. *Neuropsychopharmacology, 33,* 2791–2800. https://doi.org/10.1038/npp.2008.17

Claparède, E. (1951). Recognition and "me-ness." In D. Rapaport (Ed.), *Organization and pathology of thought* (pp. 286–292). Columbia University Press.

Compton, R. J., Carp, J., Chaddock, L., Fineman, S. L., Quandt, L. C., & Ratliff, J. B. (2008). Trouble crossing the bridge: Altered interhemispheric communication of emotional images in anxiety. *Emotion, 8*(5), 684–692. https://doi.org/10.1037/a0012910

Doidge, N. (2007). *The brain that changes itself: Stories of personal triumph from the frontiers of brain science.* Penguin.

Doll, A., Hölzel, B. K., Bratec, S. M, Boucard, C. C., Xie, X., Wohlschläger, A. M., & Sorg, C. (2016). Mindful attention to breath regulates emotions via increased amygdala–prefrontal cortex connectivity. *NeuroImage, 134,* 305–313. https://doi.org/10.1016/j.neuroimage.2016.03.041

Drake, C., Roehrs, T., Shambroom, J., & Roth, T. (2013). Caffeine effects on sleep taken 0, 3, or 6 hours before going to bed. *Journal of Clinical Sleep Medicine, 9*(11), 1195–1200. https://dx.doi.org/10.5664%2Fjcsm.3170

Ellis, A. (2016). *How to control your anxiety before it controls you.* Citadel.

Ensari, I., Greenlee, T. A., Motl, R. W., & Petruzzello, S. J. (2015). Meta-analysis of acute exercise effects on state anxiety: An update of randomized controlled trials over the past 25 years. *Depression and Anxiety, 32*(8), 624–634. https://doi.org/10.1002/da.22370

Freeston, M. H., Dugas, M. J., & Ladouceur, R. (1996). Thoughts, images, worry, and anxiety. *Cognitive Therapy and Research, 20*(3), 265–273. https://doi.org/10.1007/BF02229237

Goldin, P. R., & Gross, J. J. (2010). Effects of mindfulness-based stress reduction (MBSR) on emotion regulation in social anxiety disorder. *Emotion, 10*(1), 83–91. https://doi.org/10.1037/a0018441

Gourlay, C., Colrain, I., Chan, J., Trinder, J., & Nicholas, C. (2016). The effects of acute and chronic alcohol use on sleep architecture in male and female young adults. *Journal of Sleep Research, 25*(S2), Article O94.

Greenwood, B. N., Strong, P. V., Loughridge, A. B., Day, H. E. W., Clark, P. J., Mika, A., Hellwinkel, J. E., Spence, K. G., & Fleshner, M. (2012). 5-HT$_{2C}$ receptors in the basolateral amygdala and dorsal striatum are a novel target for the anxiolytic and antidepressant effects of exercise. *PLoS ONE, 7*(9), Article e46118. https://doi.org/10.1371/journal.pone.0046118

Grözinger, M., Beersma, D. G. M., Fell, J., & Röschke, J. (2002). Is the nonREM-REM sleep cycle reset by forced awakenings from REM sleep? *Physiological Behavior, 77*(2–3), 341–347. https://doi.org/10.1016/s0031-9384(02)00862-4

Grupe, D. W., & Nitschke, J. B. (2013). Uncertainty and anticipation in anxiety: An integrated neurobiological and psychological perspective. *Nature Reviews Neuroscience, 14,* 488–501. https://doi.org/10.1038/nrn3524

Grupe, D. W., Oathes, D. J., & Nitschke, J. B. (2013). Dissecting the anticipation of aversion reveals dissociable neural networks. *Cerebral Cortex, 23*(8), 1874–1883. https://doi.org/10.1093/cercor/bhs175

Hamm, A. O., Weike, A. I., Schupp, H. T., Treig, T., Dressel, A., & Kessler, C. (2003). Affective blindsight: Intact fear conditioning to a visual cue in a cortically blind patient. *Brain, 126*(2), 267–275. https://doi.org/10.1093/brain/awg037

Harding, E. C., Franks, N. P., & Wisden, W. (2019). The temperature dependence of sleep. *Frontiers in Neuroscience, 13,* Article 336. https://doi.org/10.3389/fnins.2019.00336

Hariri, A. R., Drabant, E. M., Munoz, K. E, Kolachana, B. S., Mattay, V. S., Egan, M. F., & Weinberger, D. R. (2005). A susceptibility gene for affective disorders and the response of the human amygdala. *Archives of General Psychiatry, 62*(2), 146–152. https://doi.org/10.1001/archpsyc.62.2.146

Havinga, P. (2020). *Breaking the cycle? Intergenerational transmission of depression/anxiety and opportunities for intervention* [Doctoral dissertation, Rijksuniversiteit Groningen]. https://doi.org/10.33612/diss.112725525

Hebb, D. O. (1949). *The organization of behavior: A neuropsychological theory.* Wiley.

Hirshkowitz, M., Whiton, K., Albert, S. M., Alessi, C., Bruni, O., DonCarlos, L., Hazen, N., Herman, J., Katz, E. S., Kheirandish-Gozal, L., Neubauer, D. N., O'Donnell, A. E., Ohayon, M., Peever, J., Rawding, R., Sachdeva, R. C., Setters, B., Vitiello, M. V., Ware, J. C., & Adams Hillard, P. J. (2015). National Sleep Foundation's sleep time duration recommendations: Methodology and results summary. *Sleep Health, 1*(1), 40–43. https://doi.org/10.1016/j.sleh.2014.12.010

Jerath, R., Barnes, V. A., Dillard-Wright, D., Jerath, S., & Hamilton, B. (2012). Dynamic change of awareness during meditation techniques: Neural and physiological correlates. *Frontiers in Human Neuroscience, 6,* Article 131. https://doi.org/10.3389/fnhum.2012.00131

Jerath, R., Crawford, M. W., Barnes, V. A., & Harden, K. (2015). Self-regulation of breathing as a primary treatment for anxiety. *Applied Psychophysiological Biofeedback, 40*(2), 107–115. https://doi.org/10.1007/s10484-015-9279-8

Kaiser Permanente. (2019). *Benzodiazepine and Z-drug safety guideline.* https://wa.kaiserpermanente.org/static/pdf/public/guidelines/benzo-zdrug.pdf

Komori, T. (2018). The relaxation effect of prolonged expiratory breathing. *Mental Illness, 10*(1), Article 7669. https://dx.doi.org/10.4081%2Fmi.2018.7669

LaBar, K. S., & Warren, L. H. (2009). Methodological approaches to studying the human amygdala. In P. J. Whalen & E. A. Phelps (Eds.), *The human amygdala* (pp. 155–176). Guilford Press.

Lack, L. C., Gradisar, M., van Someran, E. J. W., Wright, H. R., & Lushington, K. (2008). The relationship between insomnia and body temperatures. *Sleep Medicine Reviews, 12*(4), 307–317. https://doi.org/10.1016/j.smrv.2008.02.003

Lang, T. & Helbig-Lang, S. (2012). Exposure in vivo with and without presence of a therapist: Does it matter? In P. Neudeck & H.-U. Wittchen (Eds.), *Exposure therapy* (pp. 261–273). Springer.

LeDoux, J. E. (1996). *The emotional brain: The mysterious underpinnings of emotional life.* Simon & Schuster.

LeDoux, J. E. (2015). *Anxious: Using the brain to understand and treat fear and anxiety.* Viking.

Leem, Y.-H., Jang, J.-H., Park, J.-S., & Kim, H.-S. (2019). Exercise exerts an anxiolytic effect against repeated restraint stress through 5-HT$_{2A}$-mediated suppression of the adenosine A2A receptor in the basolateral amygdala. *Psychoneuroendocrinology, 108,* 182–189. https://doi.org/10.1016/j.psyneuen.2019.06.005

Maier, W., Buller, R., Philipp, M., & Heuser, I. (1988). The Hamilton Anxiety Scale: Reliability, validity, and sensitivity to change in anxiety and depressive disorders. *Journal of Affective Disorders, 14*(1), 61–68. https://doi.org/10.1016/0165-0327(88)90072-9

McNay, E. (2015). Recurrent hypoglycemia increases anxiety and amygdala norepinephrine release during subsequent hypoglycemia. *Frontiers in Endocrinology, 6,* Article 175. https://doi.org/10.3389/fendo.2015.00175

Mendes, L. P. S., Moraes, K. S., Hoffman, M., Vieira, D. S. R., Ribeiro-Samora, G. A., Lage, S. M., Britto, R. R., & Parreira, V. F. (2019). Effects of diaphragmatic breathing with and without pursed-lip breathing in subjects with COPD. *Respiratory Care, 64*(2), 136–144. https://doi.org/10.4187/respcare.06319

Milham, M. P., Nugent, A. C., Drevets, W. C., Dickstein, D. P., Leibenluft, E., Ernst, M., Charney, D., & Pine, D. S. (2005). Selective reduction in amygdala volume in pediatric anxiety disorders: A voxel-based morphometry investigation. *Biological Psychiatry, 57*(9), 961–966. https://doi.org/10.1016/j.biopsych.2005.01.038

Motomura, Y., Katsunuma, R., Yoshimura, M., & Mishima, K. (2017). Two days' sleep debt causes mood decline during resting state via diminished amygdala-prefrontal connectivity. *Sleep, 40*(10), 1–9. https://doi.org/10.1093/sleep/zsx133

Myllymäki, T., Kyröläinen, H., Savolainen, K., Hokka, L., Jakonen, R., Juuti, T., Martinmäki, K., Kaartinen, J., Kinnunen, M.-L., & Rusko, H. (2011). Effects of vigorous late-night exercise on sleep quality and cardiac autonomic activity. *Journal of Sleep Research, 20*, 146–153. https://doi.org/10.1111/j.1365-2869.2010.00874.x

National Institutes of Health. (2011). *Your guide to healthy sleep.* NIH Publication No. 11–5271. https://www.nhlbi.nih.gov/files/docs/public/sleep/healthy_sleep.pdf

Okamoto-Mizuno, K. & Mizuno, K. (2012). Effects of thermal environment on sleep and circadian rhythm. *Journal of Physiological Anthropology, 31*, Article 14. https://doi.org/10.1186/1880-6805-31-14

Pacheco, D. (2021, June 24). *The best temperature for sleep.* Sleep Foundation. https://www.sleepfoundation.org/bedroom-environment/best-temperature-for-sleep

Pal, G. K., Velkumary, S., & Madanmohan. (2004). Effect of short-term practice of breathing exercises on autonomic functions in normal human volunteers. *Indian Journal of Medical Research, 120*(2), 115–121.

Park, S.-Y., Oh, M.-K., Lee, B.-S., Kim, H.-G., Lee, W.-J., Lee, J.-H., Lim, J.-T., & Kim, J.-Y. (2015). The effects of alcohol on quality of sleep. *Korean Journal of Family Medicine, 36*(6), 294–299. https://dx.doi.org/10.4082%2Fkjfm.2015.36.6.294

Physicians' Desk Reference (71st ed.). (2016). PDR Network.

Pittman, C. M., & Karle, E. M. (2015). *Rewire your anxious brain: How to use the neuroscience of fear to end anxiety, panic & worry.* New Harbinger.

Porges, S. W. (2017). *The pocket guide to the polyvagal theory: The transformative power of feeling safe.* W. W. Norton.

Prather, A. A., Bogdan, R., & Hariri, A. R. (2013). *Impact of sleep quality on amygdala reactivity, negative affect, and perceived stress. Psychosomatic Medicine, 75*(4), 350–358. https://dx.doi.org/10.1097%2FPSY.0b013e31828ef15b

Quirk, G. J., Repa, J. C., & LeDoux, J. E. (1995). Fear conditioning enhances short-latency auditory responses of lateral amygdala neurons: Parallel recordings in the freely behaving rat. *Neuron, 15*, 1029–1039. https://doi.org/10.1016/0896-6273(95)90092-6

Raymann, R. J. E. M., & van Someren, E. J. W. (2008). Diminished capability to recognize the optimal temperature for sleep initiation may contribute to poor sleep in elderly people. *Sleep, 31*(9), 1301–1309. http://dx.doi.org/10.5665/sleep/31.9.1301

Rebar, A. L., Stanton, R., Geard, D., Short, C., Duncan, M. J., & Vandelanotte, C. (2015). A meta-meta-analysis of the effect of physical activity on depression and anxiety in non-clinical adult populations. *Health Psychology Review, 9*(3), 366–378. https://doi.org/10.1080/17437199.2015.1022901

Renna, M. E., O'Toole, M. S., Fresco, D. M., Heimberg, R. G., & Mennin, D. S. (2021). From psychological to physical health: Exploring temporal precedence throughout emotion regulation therapy. *Journal of Anxiety Disorders, 80*, Article 102403. https://doi.org/10.1016/j.janxdis.2021.102403

Roehrs, T., & Roth, T. (2008). Caffeine: Sleep and daytime sleepiness. *Sleep Medicine Reviews, 12*(2), 153–162. https://doi.org/10.1016/j.smrv.2007.07.004

Rogers, P. J. (2007). Caffeine, mood and mental performance in everyday life. *Nutrition Bulletin, 32*(S1), 84–89. https://doi.org/10.1111/j.1467-3010.2007.00607.x

Rogers, P. J., Heatherley, S. V., Mullings, E. L., & Nutt, D. J. (2006). Licit drug use and depression, anxiety and stress. *Journal of Psychopharmacology, 20*(Suppl.), A27.

Rothbaum, B. O., Price, M., Jovanovic, T., Norrholm, S. D., Gerardi, M., Dunlop, B., Davis, M., Bradley, B., Duncan, E. J., Rizzo, A., & Ressler, K. J. (2014). A randomized, double-blind evaluation of D-cycloserine or alprazolam combined with virtual reality exposure therapy for posttraumatic stress disorder in Iraq and Afghanistan war veterans. *American Journal of Psychiatry, 171*(6), 640–648. https://doi.org/10.1176/appi.ajp.2014.13121625

Roy, M. J., Costanzo, M. E., Blair, J. R., & Rizzo, A. A. (2014). Compelling evidence that exposure therapy for PTSD normalizes brain function. In B. K. Wiederhold & G. Riva (Eds.), *Annual review of cybertherapy and telemedicine* (pp. 61–65). IOS Press.

Sahraie, A., Weiskrantz, L., Barbur, J. L., Simmons, A., Williams, S. C. R., & Brammer, M. J. (1997). Pattern of neuronal activity associated with conscious and unconscious processing of visual signals. *PNAS, 94*, 9406–9411. https://doi.org/10.1073/pnas.94.17.9406

Schwartz, J. M., & Begley, S. (2003). *The mind and the brain: Neuroplasticity and the power of mental force.* HarperCollins.

Sircar, M., Bhatia, A., & Munshi, M. (2016). Review of hypoglycemia in the older adult: Clinical implications and management. *Canadian Journal of Diabetes, 40*(1), 66–72. https://doi.org/10.1016/j.jcjd.2015.10.004

Smith, J. E., Lawrence, A. D., Diukova, A., Wise, R. G., & Rogers, P. J. (2012). Storm in a coffee cup: Caffeine modifies brain activation to social signals of threat. *SCAN, 7*(7), 831–840. https://dx.doi.org/10.1093%2Fscan%2Fnsr058

Stutz, J., Eiholzer, R., & Spengler, C. M. (2019). Effects of evening exercise on sleep in healthy participants: A systematic review and meta-analysis. *Sports Medicine, 49*(2), 269–287. https://doi.org/10.1007/s40279-018-1015-0

Sudak, D. M. (2011). *Combining CBT and medication: An evidence-based approach.* Wiley.

Suni, E. (2020, December 3). *Sleeping pills: Medications & prescription sleep aids.* Sleep Foundation. https://www.sleepfoundation.org/sleep-medications

Trauer, J. M., Qian, M. Y., Doyle, J. S., Rajaratnam, S. M. W., & Cunnington, D. (2015). Cognitive behavioral therapy for chronic insomnia: A systematic review and meta-analysis. *Annals of Internal Medicine, 163*(3), 191–204. https://doi.org/10.7326/m14-2841

Trockel, M., Manber, R., Chang, V., Thurston, A., & Tailor, C. B. (2011). An e-mail delivered CBT for sleep-health program for college students: Effects on sleep quality and depression symptoms. *Journal of Clinical Sleep Medicine, 7*(3), 276–281. https://dx.doi.org/10.5664%2FJCSM.1072

Tully, P. J., Cosh, S. M., & Baune, B. T. (2013). A review of the affects [*sic*] of worry and generalized anxiety disorder upon cardiovascular health and coronary heart disease. *Psychology, Health & Medicine, 18*(6), 627–644. https://doi.org/10.1080/13548506.2012.749355

Uhde, T. W., Roy-Byrne, P., Gillin, J. C., Mendelson, W. B., Boulenger, J.-P., Vittone, B. J., & Post, R. M. (1984). The sleep of patients with panic disorder: A preliminary report. *Psychiatry Research, 12*(3), 251–259. https://doi.org/10.1016/0165-1781(84)90030-1

van der Helm, E., Yao, J., Dutt, S., Rao, V., Saletin, J. M., & Walker, M. P. (2011). REM sleep de-potentiates amygdala activity to previous emotional experiences. *Current Biology, 21*(23), 2029–2032. https://dx.doi.org/10.1016%2Fj.cub.2011.10.052

van Minnen, A., Arntz, A., & Keijsers, G. P. J. (2002). Prolonged exposure in patients with chronic PTSD: Predictors of treatment outcome and dropout. *Behavior Research and Therapy, 40*(4), 439–457. https://doi.org/10.1016/s0005-7967(01)00024-9

Van Reen, E., Jenni, O. G., & Carskadon, M. A. (2006). Effects of alcohol on sleep and the sleep electroencephalogram in healthy young women. *Alcoholism: Clinical and Experimental Research, 30*(6), 974–981. https://doi.org/10.1111/j.1530-0277.2006.00111.x

Veleber, D. M., & Templer, D. I. (1984). Effects of caffeine on anxiety and depression. *Journal of Abnormal Psychology, 93*(1), 120–122. https://doi.org/10.1037/0021-843X.93.1.120

Verduyn, P., Van Mechelen, I., & Tuerlinckx, F. (2011). The relation between event processing and the duration of emotional experience. *Emotion, 11*(1), 20–28. https://doi.org/10.1037/a0021239

Verkuil, B., Brosschot, J. F., Borkovec, T. D., & Thayer, J. F. (2009). Acute autonomic effects of experimental worry and cognitive problem solving: Why worry about worry? *International Journal of Clinical and Health Psychology, 9*(3), 439–453.

Vuilleumier, P. (2009). The role of the human amygdala in perception and attention. In P. J. Whalen & E. A. Phelps (Eds.), *The Human Amygdala* (pp. 220–249). Guilford Press.

Wams, E. J., Woelders, T., Marring, I., van Rosmalen, L., Beersma, D. G. M., Gordijn, M. C. M., & Hut, R. A. (2017). Linking light exposure and subsequent sleep: A field polysomnography study in humans. *Sleep, 40*(12), Article zsx165. https://doi.org/10.1093/sleep/zsx165

Watson, E. J., Coates, A. M., Kohler, M., & Banks, S. (2016). Caffeine consumption and sleep quality in Australian adults. *Nutrients, 8*(8), 479. https://doi.org/10.3390/nu8080479

Wilson, R. (2016). *Stopping the noise in your head: The new way to overcome anxiety and worry.* Health Communications, Inc.

Yoo, S.-S., Gujar, N., Hu, P., Jolesz, F. A., & Walker, M. P. (2007). The human emotional brain without sleep—a prefrontal amygdala disconnect. *Current Biology, 17*(20), 877–878. https://doi.org/10.1016/j.cub.2007.08.007

Youngstedt, S. D., & Kline, C. E. (2006). Epidemiology of exercise and sleep. *Sleep and Biological Rhythms, 4*(3), 215–221. https://dx.doi.org/10.1111%2Fj.1479-8425.2006.00235.x

Zaccaro, A., Piarulli, A., Laurino, M., Garbella, E., Menicucci, D., Neri, B., & Gemignani, A. (2018). How breath control can change your life: A systematic review on psycho-physiological correlates of slow breathing. *Frontiers in Human Neuroscience, 12*, Article 353. https://doi.org/10.3389/fnhum.2018.00353

Zhou, L., Podolsky, N., Sang, Z., Ding, Y., Fan, X., Tong, Q., Levin, B. E., & McCrimmon, R. J. (2010). The medial amygdalar nucleus: A novel glucose-sensing region that modulates the counterregulatory response to hypoglycemia. *Diabetes, 59*(10), 2646–2652. https://dx.doi.org/10.2337%2Fdb09-0995

Ziemann, A. E., Allen, J. E., Dahdaleh, N. S., Drebot, I. I., Coryell, M. W., Wunsch, A. M., Lynch, C. M., Faraci, F. M., Howard, M. A., Welsh, M. J., & Wemmie, J. A. (2009). The amygdala is a chemosensor that detects carbon dioxide and acidosis to elicit fear behavior. *Cell, 139*(5), 1012–1021. https://doi.org/10.1016/j.cell.2009.10.029

Made in the USA
Monee, IL
05 May 2024

58028459R00096